Collins

easy learning
Writing

The easiest way to accurate and effective writing

HarperCollins Publishers
Westerhill Road
Bishopbriggs
Glasgow
G64 2QT

Second edition 2015
Latest Reprinted Indian edition 2016
10 9 8 7 6 5 4 3 2 1

ISBN 978-8-17-223675-5

www.collinsdictionary.com/cobuild
www.collinselt.com
www.collins.in

A catalogue record for this book is available from the British Library

Typeset by Davidson Publishing Solutions, Glasgow

Printed in India by MicroPrints India

Editorial staff

Written by:
Elizabeth Walter and Kate Woodford

Editor: Lisa Sutherland

For the publisher:
Lucy Cooper
Kerry Ferguson
Elaine Higgleton
Celia Wigley

introduction

Collins Easy Learning Writing is suitable for anyone who wants to write clear, elegant English, whether at school, at home or at work. It is written in a simple, clear way, with lots of examples showing how the guidance given can be put into practice.

The book has three main parts:

The first part deals with the things you need to know before you can write effectively. The topics covered here apply to all types of writing, and range from planning your writing to checking it at the end. There are sections on the best way to present your writing on the page, on how to structure longer documents, and on many tricky issues such as how to write speech, abbreviations, numbers and more. In addition, there is a comprehensive section on style, covering areas such as writing plain English, avoiding ambiguity and writing with the appropriate level of formality.

The second part takes a detailed look at different types of writing, from informal emails and letters to formal essays, reports and presentations. It gives advice on structure, tone and style, and examples of good practice, as well as providing suggestions for useful words and phrases to use in your own work.

The third part covers grammar, punctuation and spelling. It gives the basic rules you need to know and draws attention to common mistakes and shows you how to avoid them.

We hope *Collins Easy Learning Writing* will help you to write with confidence and success. For more information on products to help you improve your English, please visit us at **www.collinselt.com**.

contents

contents

Preparing to write

PART ONE

Thinking about your writing

Whatever you are writing, it is important to think about it first. If you plan your writing well, it will be **clear, logical and effective**.

You may think that planning your writing is just one extra job, and a waste of time, but in fact good planning will probably **save you time** as well as making your writing better.

Planning does not necessarily take a lot of time, and you do not always need to make a **written plan**. For instance, it would be silly to make a written plan for a text message – the whole point is that texting is a quick way of communicating. However, even with a text message, you should plan **in your mind**, so that you know what you want to say.

For longer pieces of writing, such as essays, reports, and often even letters, it is very useful to make a written plan. A plan will help you:

- *organize your thoughts*
- *make sure you are clear about what you want to write*
- *make sure you have all the information you need*
- *make sure you don't leave anything out*

Key point to remember
Planning will save you time and make your writing more effective.

Before you start to write, the most important question to ask yourself is: **What am I trying to achieve?**

The best way to be clear about this is to ask three questions:

1 **Who** is this writing for?
2 **What** do I want to say?
3 **Why** do I want to say it?

Imagine, for example, that you really like animals, and you need a holiday job, so you decide to write to the local zoo. In this case, the answers to the questions above could be:

1 The manager or personnel officer of the zoo.
2 That you want a summer holiday job. That you love animals and worked on a farm last year.
3 Because you want to get a holiday job in a zoo.

There are important points to remember about each of these questions:

- **Who?** Make sure that you use a suitable style and tone for your audience. Informal language and jokes are fine for your friends, but a job application needs to be more formal.
- **What?** Make sure that what you say is absolutely clear, and that you have included everything you wanted to include.
- **Why?** Make sure the letter achieves what you want it to achieve. For instance, if you write a letter of complaint, be clear about what you want to happen: are you writing it because you want an apology, or do you want your money back?

Before starting to write, it can sometimes be helpful to make a brief summary of what you are trying to achieve. This can help you to concentrate on the most important points of your writing.

When you have finished your writing, you can go back to your summary and check that what you have written achieves what you wanted it to. A good summary will always answer the questions, who?, what? and why?

Here are two examples of this kind of summary:

A survey of students' opinions of the food in our school canteen, to be used as the basis of a campaign for better school meals.

A letter of complaint to the manager of the local theatre to say that our recent visit was spoiled by the noise of building work going on in the bar area, and to ask for our money back.

Your summary can also help you resist the temptation to add too many details or extra points. Remember that many people are busy – if they do not understand your main points quickly, you may not achieve what you hope to achieve.

Key point to remember
Always be clear about the purpose of your writing.

Organizing your ideas

Whatever you are planning to write, you need to organize your ideas, either on paper, on your computer, or in your head.

There are several good things about this stage of writing:

- You do not need to worry about grammar and spelling
- You do not need to write whole sentences: single words, phrases, or even pictures are fine
- You do not need to put your ideas into any kind of order to begin with – that can come later
- The act of writing things down can give you new ideas

It is also fine to write down things that you don't know!

Say, for instance, you are writing an essay about the causes of the First World War, a subject you have been studying in class. You might write down the things you know about, e.g. the Alliances between different countries, the assassination of Archduke Franz Ferdinand, the struggle between Britain and Germany to have military control of the seas.

Then you can add things you do not know, but think you ought to include in your essay. Examples might be: why were these Alliances formed?; who killed Franz Ferdinand and why?; what role did imperialism play in the arguments between countries?

These **questions** will help you to see what **further research** you need to do.

Tip for success
If you write down your ideas, you will not forget them!

When you have written down all your ideas, you need to put them in some kind of **order**. If you have a very clear idea of what your writing will contain, it may be possible to do this right from the beginning.

One simple way to order your ideas is to list them under different **headings**.

For instance, this writer is planning an article for her student magazine about working holidays abroad:

Reasons to work abroad	***Types of work available***	***Practical issues***
chance to travel *see 'real' life* *earn money* *make new friends* *work experience*	*voluntary v. paid* *teaching* *farm work* *tourist industry*	*legal: work permits, etc.* *safety* *cheapest way to travel there* *how much will you earn?*

It can be useful to be able to **move your ideas around**.

One possibility is to use **Post-it® notes** (small pieces of paper with one sticky edge) and arrange them on a table or a wall.

Imagine you are writing a party invitation. You want to include the date and time of the party, what it's celebrating, that you need a reply to your invitation, that friends and partners are welcome and that you'd like people to bring drinks.

If you write all those things on Post-it® notes, you can make sure you include all the points you want to, and in the best order.

A very flexible way of ordering ideas is to use **mind maps**, or **spider maps**. In these maps, you start with the most important, central idea, and work out from there, using branches leading outwards. The more detailed the idea, the further the branches are from the central point.

This writer is planning to write a leaflet about what we can do to protect the environment:

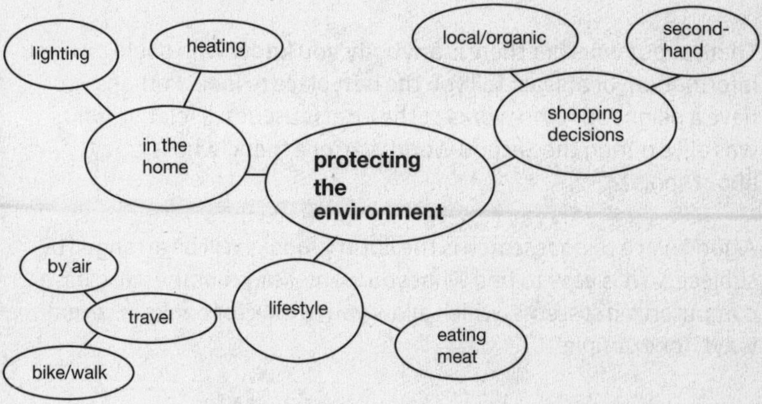

Tip for success
A good mind map will help you structure your writing by showing you how points relate to each other.

Research

For some pieces of writing, especially longer pieces, you will need to do some research. How much you need to do will depend on the information you already have and the amount of detail your writing needs.

If you are a student, your **teacher** will be able to help. They may give you a list of books or websites to use.

Think about whether there is **anybody you know** who could give you information, or at least tell you the best place to look. Perhaps you have a neighbour who works at the local museum, a relative who was alive during the Second World War, or a friend who is crazy about sport?

A good place to do research is the **library**. Books will be arranged by subject, so it is easy to find what you want. Many libraries also have computerized systems, which allow you to look for books in several ways, for example:

- by subject
- by keywords in the title
  (important words that give a clue to what the book is about)
- by author
- by date of publication

It is often useful to ask the **librarians** for help. They will know about all the different sources of information, some of which may not be in book form. For example, many libraries have copies of old newspapers in a photographed form, which you need a special machine to read.

Remember that it is often possible to use a library's website to search for books from wherever you are, rather than having to go to the library to do so.

Libraries also have a large amount of information stored electronically. For instance, many existing books have been converted to **e-books**, and some new books are *only* published in this way. Similarly, **e-magazines** exist alongside or instead of paper versions. Many newspapers are available electronically too, making searching for items much easier.

For academic research, you will often need to refer to **journals**. Public libraries will stock some important journals, but university libraries will have many more.

These days, many academic journals are published as **online journals** only. These are available for personal use by paying a subscription or by a pay-per-view system in which you pay a small amount each time you use them.

However, many public libraries have access to important online journals, and you can use them free of charge from a computer in the library. You should be aware that most libraries have a time limit for computer use, so it is best to be sure of the information you want to find before you start.

Universities will have a wider range of specialist online journals and e-books, and most will have a system that allows you to access them from wherever you want to.

Using the Internet is a quick and useful way to research a topic. However, it is important to remember that **absolutely anyone** can put information on a website. You need to make sure that any source you use is suitable.

A good starting point is to ask two questions:

- **Who** wrote the information you are looking at?
- **What** is the purpose of the site where you found it?

Answering these questions will help you to think about two further questions:

- Is this information likely to be reliable?
- Is the information likely to be fair, or does the writer have a particular purpose, such as supporting an opinion or trying to make you buy something?

Using a **search engine** such as Google® or Yahoo® can be a start, but there is a danger that you find so many sites that you miss the ones which are really important. There are several ways to make your searches more effective, for example:

- Try to make your search item as specific as possible.
- If you put your search items in double inverted commas (" ") the search engine will look for the words in exactly that form. This can be useful, for example, for searching for someone's name.
- Search engines often have special options, for example to restrict a search to sites from a particular region, or to information from a particular time period.

Many teachers and lecturers include websites on their reading lists, so if you have been given a reading list, make sure you use it. Otherwise, think about sites that will be reliable. For instance, in the UK you might look for medical information on the National Health Service site. In Australia, you might look for news information on the ABC site.

Tip for success
If you are using the Internet in a library, the librarian may be able to help you find suitable sites.

Making notes and summaries

When you are doing research, you will want to **make notes**. Your notes can be in whatever form suits you best. The important thing is to make sure you will still understand them when you come to use them!

Do make sure that the notes you take **relate to the subject** you will be writing about. There is no point adding extra information – however interesting it is – that you will not be able to use.

Notes should be **short** – do not copy out huge pieces of text. In order to **summarize**, it is very important to make sure you have understood the main points. When you have read a chapter or an article, it can be useful to try to write down the most important three or four points in it.

Look for clues in what you are reading to help you:

- Are there any words that are <u>underlined</u> or in **heavy type**?
- Do the headings summarize the main points?
- Does the book itself include summaries or lists of main points?

Do use abbreviations, shorten words or miss out words altogether. 'Romans > Britain 55BC' is much more efficient than writing 'The Romans came to Britain in 55BC.'

> **Key point to remember**
> Make sure you will be able to understand your notes when you need to use them.

If you have a good idea of the structure of your piece of writing, it can be useful to organize your notes.

For example, if you are writing an essay about a book you have read, you may be asked to look at particular things, such as the way the author builds up characters; the style of language used; the way the plot develops; the author's relationship with the reader.

If you divide your paper into **themes** like these, you can order your notes as you take them. This will make it easier to organize your essay, and also help you balance the amounts of material you have on each theme.

You may use your notes to record good **quotations** to use in your own writing, but be careful:

- If you use a direct quotation, you must produce it accurately, and you must say where it has come from.
- If you summarize what someone has said, you must change it into your **own words**. Copying the words of others is called **plagiarizing**. It is not allowed in academic work, and it can be illegal.

Tip for success
While you are making notes, keep a list of **useful words and phrases** to use in your own writing.

Outlines

For longer pieces of writing, it is useful to produce an outline before you start. An outline can have as much or as little in it as you think will be useful for you, but it should at least include a basic list of **headings**. If you have organized your ideas and notes in some of the ways suggested above, you will probably find it quite easy to produce an outline.

Start by picking out a number of main points – these will be the main frame for your writing, and will lead to more detailed points within them.

For some types of writing, such as a report, it may be appropriate to keep these headings in the final text. For others, the headings will simply be a way of organizing your writing and will not appear in your finished work.

You can use your outline to check that everything you want to write is in a **logical order**:

- Make sure that understanding one part does not rely on another part that comes later
- If you move on to a different point, see if it needs some sort of introduction or explanation
- Make sure that all the points connected to a particular theme are treated together

The person who made this outline is writing a report on the use of volunteers in a local charity:

Volunteer report

Introduction

- What this report covers
- Research and methods used
- Purpose of report

Summary of main points

The current situation

- number of volunteers
- what they do
- how they are managed

Problems with the current situation

- not enough volunteers
- volunteers not clear about their role
- lack of communication with paid staff

Suggestions for improvement

- better targeting of recruitment campaigns
- written handbook for volunteers
- regular staff/volunteer meetings

Conclusion

Key point to remember
Use your outline to make sure everything is included and in the best order.

Writing a draft

A draft is a rough version of your finished writing. It can be as close to or as far away from the final text as you like. For instance, you may decide to concentrate on the content and not worry about spelling and punctuation – that is up to you.

If you are writing something very long, or very important, you may write **more than one draft**.

When you have written a draft, it is useful to ask the following questions:

- Does the **order** of what is written make sense?
- Have you **included everything** you wanted to include?
- Is all the material **relevant**? Is there anything you should cut out?
- Is the **tone** right? For instance, if it is a letter of complaint, is it firm and assertive or is it offensive and rude?
- Does any part need **more explanation**, more information or more evidence?
- Is the amount of **space given to each theme** appropriate, or is one part too long or too short?
- Does it **achieve** what you want it to achieve (if you wrote a brief summary at the beginning, you can check against it)?

It can sometimes be useful to give a draft of your writing to **someone else**, and ask if what you have written is clear, interesting, and effective. That person might make suggestions for additions or improvements, or check facts for you.

Key point to remember
Do not expect to produce a perfect piece of writing first time. Many people write two or more drafts of an important piece of writing before they are satisfied with it.

Presentation

General layout

A clear and attractive layout will make your texts both more enjoyable to read and easier to understand.

The use of computers makes it easy for everyone to present their writing in a professional way, and gives us lots of choices about how to do this. One of the most useful things about using a computer is that you can edit text and move it around as you work. You can experiment with different ways of presenting it – you do not have to decide on your layout at the beginning.

Here are some general rules:

- Almost all documents look better if there is plenty of **space** around the words
- Do not make your **sentences or paragraphs** too long
- Do not make the **size of type** too small
- Whatever style you choose for the different parts of your document, make sure you **keep to the same style all the way through**

Tip for success
Before you finish your document, look at it using the **print preview** option, to see how it will look on the page when it is printed.

Look at the following piece of text:

> To: all football club members
> Welcome back to football practice after the summer break. Many of you will know that we have a new kit this season. Each player will need a red shirt and shorts for home games and a blue shirt and shorts for away games, white socks with red stripes, shin pads, a tracksuit for practice which doesn't need to be in the club colours, and studded boots, which can be of any type. Please remind your parents that there is a £25 fee to cover coaching and transport to matches. See you at training next week,
> From: Matt (team coach)

Now see how a better layout can make the same information much easier to read:

> To: all football club members
>
> Welcome back to football practice after the summer break.
>
> **New kit**
> Many of you will know that we have a new kit this season. Each player will need:
>
> - red shirt and shorts (for home games)
> - blue shirt and shorts (for away games)
> - white socks with red stripes
> - shin pads
> - track suit (any colour – for practice only)
> - studded boots (any type)
>
> **Fees**
> Please remind your parents that there is a £25 fee to cover coaching and transport to matches.
>
> See you at training next week!
>
> Matt (team coach)

Most pieces of text are divided into paragraphs. Each paragraph discusses one point or idea.

The beginning of a new paragraph can be shown in two ways. The first is to **indent** the first sentence, which means starting it further to the right than the rest of the paragraph, like this:

> Additional research has shown a strong link between smoking and heart disease. In a study of more than 1,000 healthy males, it ...

The second way is to **leave a whole line of space** between paragraphs. If you do this, you do not need to indent the first sentence. Separating paragraphs in this way can help to make the structure of your writing clear by showing where each new point or idea starts and ends.

Try not to leave just one or two lines of a paragraph at the **end of a page**, or to have the last line or two of a paragraph at the **top of a page**. It is better to have a larger space than usual at the bottom of a page than to have a small part of the paragraph on its own.

> **Key point to remember**
> Using plenty of white space will make your document easier to read.

You will need to decide how you want the **edges** of your text to look.

> You can set your computer like this, so that the
> ends of the sentences do not fall in a straight line.
> This can look natural, and the spacing between
> each word looks better.

> Alternatively, you can set your computer so that the words form a neat, straight line at both of the edges. For some types of writing, this can look neater, but you may find that you get large gaps between some words in order to make them fit.

You will also have to decide whether or not you want your document to use **hyphens** if a long word comes at the end of a line. If the lines in your document are fairly long, and you are not using extremely long words, it is usually best not to use hyphens. However, if you have short lines, you may need to use them to avoid large spaces between words, especially if you are using straight lines at the edges of your text.

Hyphens must be used at a suitable breaking point in the word. Your computer will do this for you, but if you are writing by hand, you will need to decide where to put hyphens yourself. If you are not confident about this, it is best not to use them at all.

Tip for success
If you do use hyphens, check the line ends when you have finished to make sure there are no word breaks that could cause confusion, such as leg-end, or thin-king.

Fonts and typefaces

A font is the design of the letters that you use to write with. You will be able to choose fonts when you write documents on your computer. They range from standard fonts that you might use for an essay or a letter, to very unusual and dramatic ones that you might use for example for a party invitation:

> Dear Ms Hodges
> I am writing to enquire about the possibility of work experience in your company ...

> Come to our spooky ghost party!

The **normal font size** for general texts such as essays is 11 or 12 points. You may want to use larger fonts for headings. Sometimes smaller sizes (usually 10 or 11 points) are used for long quotations.

Fonts like this one, which have very small lines at the ends of letters, are called **serif** fonts, while fonts like this one, which have nothing at the ends, are called **sans-serif** fonts. It is best to use a serif font such as 'Times New Roman' for long pieces of text.

You can also choose different ways of writing words, for example using *italics*, **bold (also called heavy) type**, underlining, or SMALL CAPITALS.

> **Tip for success**
> Avoid writing more than a few words in CAPITAL LETTERS because they are difficult to read.

Bullet points

If you want to separate out a list of points from the main part of your text, a simple way to do so is to use bullet points.

Bullet points are often used when the order of the list is not particularly important, e.g.:

> During this exciting week-long course, students will:
>
> - learn how to gather food in the wild
> - spend two nights in a nearby forest
> - learn how to build a shelter from earth and branches

It is not usual to use full stops at the end of bullet points, though if the points themselves are more than one sentence, you may feel it looks better.

You can decide whether or not to use capital letters at the beginning of each bullet point. In the example above, capital letters were not used because each bullet point formed a complete sentence following the introductory phrase 'students will ...'.

> **Key point to remember**
> The most important thing to remember is that when you have decided whether or not to use capital letters and full stops, you should do the same for each point.

Bullet points can be introduced by any sort of symbol you think is appropriate:

- ● Probably the most common type is a circle like this
- – A dash is also an acceptable way to introduce a point

- ▶ You may want to emphasize your point more with a symbol like this
- ♪ Or even choose something completely different if it is relevant to your text

It is important to make sure that the bullet points match up grammatically with the words you use to introduce them. If you use a phrase such as '*You will need the following:*', it is simple to follow it by a list of items.

However, you will often find bullet points introduced by phrases such as:

> *To write a successful essay, you should:*
> *Students will have the opportunity to:*

In cases like this, make sure you read through the introductory phrase and the bullet point together, to make certain they form a correct sentence. Look at the following:

> Students will have the opportunity to:
>
> - canoe in the local river
> - learn how to cook on a camp fire
> - making lots of new friends

The third point does not make a grammatically correct sentence, and should be 'make lots of new friends'.

Numbered points

Numbered points are used in a similar way to bullet points, but are often used to show that the order of points is important:

The most common UK girls' names in 2014 were:

1. Sophia
2. Emily
3. Lily
4. Olivia
5. Amelia

You can use numbers or letters to order your points, and in some cases you may even want to do both, in order to go into more detail about a particular point:

Here is the agenda for Monday's meeting:

1. Minutes of the last meeting
2. Sales reports
    a. Europe and the Middle East
    b. Americas
    c. East Asia
3. Next year's training budget
    a. in-house training
    b. external courses

Tip for success
When you want to indent a list of points, always use a function such as the **Tab key** or the bullet points or numbers from the **menu bar**. Do not try to indent using the space bar because the spacing will not be even.

Headers, footers and page numbers

Headers and footers are pieces of text that appear at the top or bottom of the pages of your document but are separate from the rest of the writing on that page.

Typical items that might be put in them include:

- document title
- chapter or section titles
- author name
- copyright information
- date
- document reference

Using headers and footers can make your work look more professional. If you have the same header and footer throughout the whole document, you only need to put the text in once.

It is also possible to use different headers and footers for different sections of a document, for example for each new chapter or section. This can be useful for readers.

Page numbers can also be added automatically, and placed wherever you want them: at the top or bottom of the page; on the right, left or in the centre.

You can also choose the position, size, font etc. of your headers and footers. For example, you may want a chapter heading at the top of each page to be quite large, but a copyright note at the bottom to be quite small.

Using images

Using images can be a great way to liven up your text. Reasons for using images may include:

- helping to explain something – sometimes an image can be clearer than words
- decorating a document such as a party invitation
- emphasizing a brand, for example by using a company logo

A simple way to get images is to use **Clip Art** that is available in your word processing software.

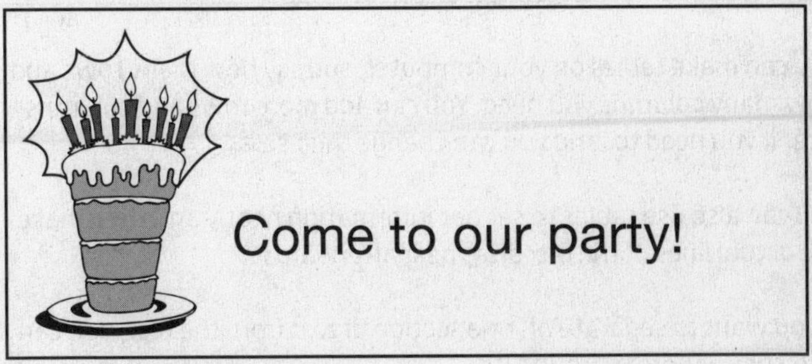

If you are using images in a more serious document, you should give them captions, and it will often be necessary to number them so that you can refer to them in the text.

Make sure that your images are an appropriate size for your document – it is easy to change the size of an image on your computer.

> **Key point to remember**
> If you use an image, make sure you are legally allowed to do so. Some images have **copyright**, which means you need the owner's permission to use them, and you may have to pay.

Tables and boxes

If you want to present information in rows and columns, it is a good idea to use a table:

Course timetable

	Group 1	*Group 2*
9.00 -9.30 9.30 – 11.00 11.00- 11.30	*Introductions* *Singing workshop* *Break*	*Introductions* *African drumming* *Break*

You can make tables on your computer, and say how many rows and how many columns you need. You can add more rows and columns later if you need to, and you can change their size.

You can also use tables to set out information neatly and then make the actual lines of the box disappear afterwards.

If you want to separate off one section of text from the rest, you can put a box or border around it.

You can also put a shade or a coloured tint inside a box to make it stand out, like this.

There are many different types of boxes and borders to choose from. This one, for example, has a shadow effect.

Charts and diagrams

Charts and diagrams can be a good way to present information, particularly numerical information, which can be much easier to understand when shown in this way.

Charts and diagrams are particularly good for information that needs to be analyzed, for example information showing **comparisons**, **patterns and trends**.

All charts and diagrams should be numbered and have a heading. Make sure there is plenty of space around them, and that there is always a reference to them in the text:

> As we can see from table 1 ...

> Fig. 3.8 illustrates the increase in ...

There are many different types of chart and diagram. Think about which one best suits the information you want to present.

Graphs

Graphs such as this one are a good way of showing trends in numbers:

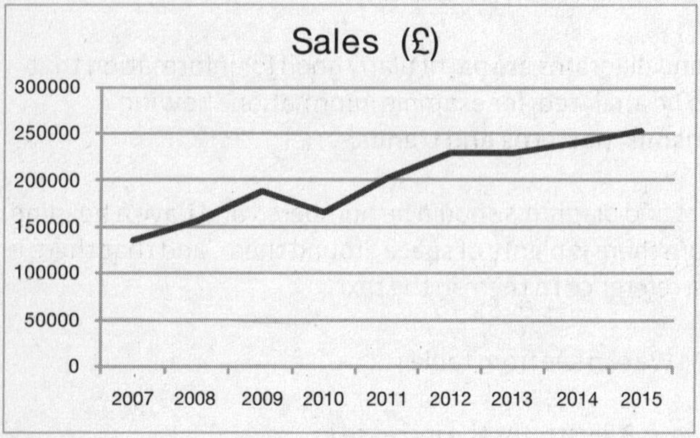

Pie charts

Pie charts are a very clear way of showing the relative size of groups of things:

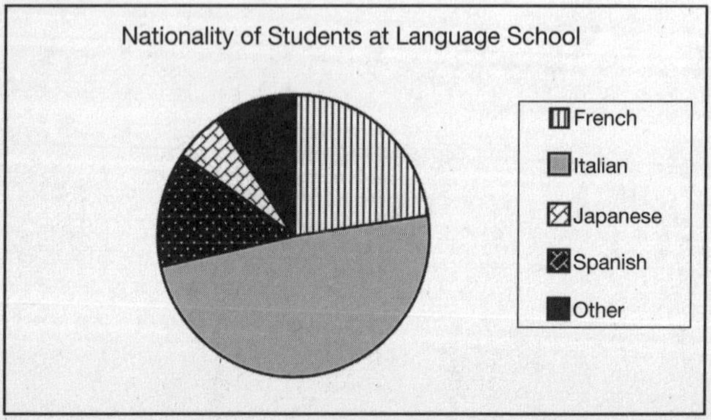

Venn Diagrams

Venn diagrams are used to show overlapping groups:

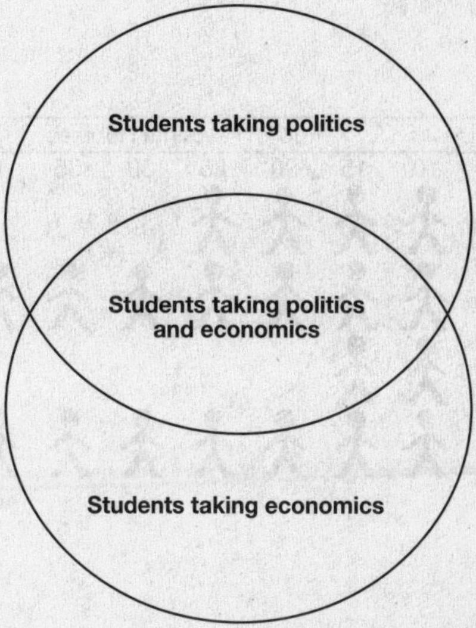

Bar charts

Bar charts also make it easy to compare numbers and amounts:

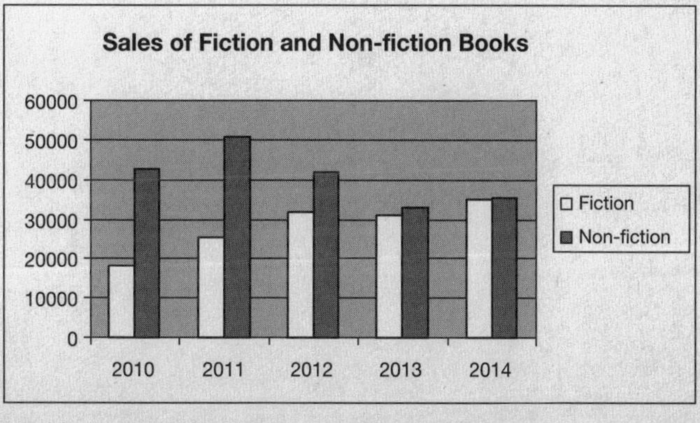

Pictograms

Pictograms are a simple way of showing numbers of people or things. As in this case, each image can represent more than one person or thing:

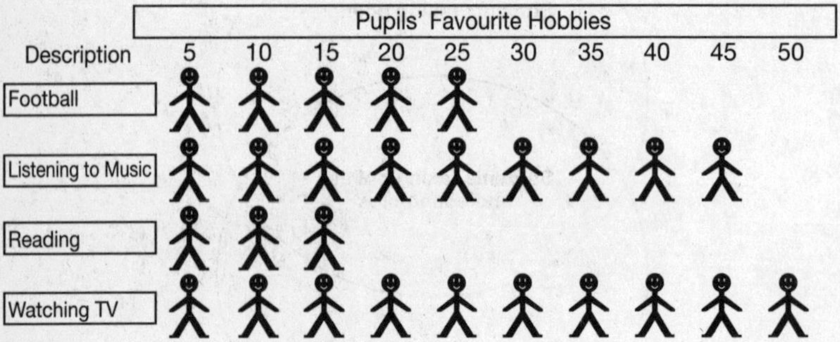

Structure

Logical ordering

If you have planned your writing well, you should have no problem writing it in a logical sequence.

Make sure that your **points lead on to each other** in such a way that your reader is guided through your argument. Remember that you should move from general points to more specific, detailed points.

Never include a point without any necessary **background or explanation**, or one that relies on reading something later in the text. Unless you actually refer to other sources, or unless you know that your reader possesses certain knowledge, the text should include all the information needed to understand it.

Make sure that all points of discussion about a particular area of your text come together – **do not change from one topic to another** and then back again.

An essay should **start with an introduction and end with a conclusion**, and in fact there are many types of writing where this is a useful principle, even if it is not done in such a formal way.
For instance, if you are writing a formal letter, it can sometimes be helpful to include a short title after the greeting. This acts as an introduction.

Introductions

When you write an essay, you should start with an **introduction** and end with a **conclusion**.

Your introduction will give your readers the information they need to lead them into the main part of the essay.

The introduction should do the following things:

- **Introduce the topic**: briefly describe what the essay is about, providing any necessary explanation of the background and context of the topic.

- **Explain the purpose of the essay**: say what you will discuss, making sure that it fits exactly with the title of your essay. If you have been given a title, be careful to look for words like 'examine', 'contrast', 'describe' or 'analyze' and make sure that this is what your essay does.

- **Define your terms**: if there is any possibility of doubt, say exactly what you mean by words and phrases, both in the title and throughout the essay. For instance, if your essay is about childhood diabetes, you should say what age range you consider to be covered by the term 'childhood'.

In the same way, if there is any possible doubt about the meaning of the title, you should say very clearly what you understand by it, and how this understanding will form the basis of what follows.

- **Explain how your points are organized**: give a very brief summary of the structure of your essay.

An introduction can be more than one paragraph, if necessary. As a general rule, it should be around 10% of the total length of your essay. Remember though, it should not be a summary of the whole thing – if it is, the reader will not bother reading to the end!

Other points you may want to cover in your introduction include:

- **A statement of why your topic is particularly interesting or important**.
- **An explanation of how your work fits into a wider context**: for example how it relates to research being done by others, or how it is affected by current events or attitudes.
- **A discussion of areas of your topic where there is a lack of knowledge**.

Tip for success
While a short quotation can be an interesting way to start an essay, avoid long quotations or detailed examples in your introduction.

Conclusions

The introduction and conclusion form a frame for your essay. The conclusion brings together all the ideas and information you have discussed. It shows the reader that the essay is complete and that the aims of the essay have been achieved.

When you write your conclusion, always look back at the introduction. Make sure that your conclusion shows your essay has really done what you said it would do.

A conclusion does two main things:

- **Summarizes** the main points and ideas.
- **Reaches conclusions** by saying what the consequences of your evidence are.

By summarizing the main points, you provide your reader with a brief, clear statement of the most important points you have discussed. You should also include a brief reminder of the purpose of this discussion.

Everything that you summarize must be fully covered in the main part of the essay – you should not add any new information here.

As well as summarizing what you have discussed, you should summarize what you have said your evidence suggests.

Key point to remember
Never add any new points or ideas in your conclusion.

The type of conclusions you reach will depend on the question you were dealing with in the essay. You might:

- **Achieve a task set in the title**: For instance, if you were asked to contrast the characters of the Bennett sisters in the novel *Pride and Prejudice*, you would simply summarize the main differences you had found.

- **Give your opinion**: For instance, if you were asked to say whether or not nuclear power is a good form of fuel, you would express your opinion and explain briefly how the evidence you have presented supports it.

- **Show what you have learned from looking at evidence**: For instance, if you are asked to analyze the results of a research project on the effects of diet on rates of heart disease, you would summarize the main facts you have discovered from the survey.

- **Make recommendations**: For instance, if you are writing a report on the best way to encourage recycling, you would suggest actions that could be taken.

Often you will find that issues you discuss in essays are complicated and you cannot find a simple answer or give a definite opinion. This is fine – you should simply explain why this is the case by summarizing the main points.

Headings

Headings are often used in long documents. They can **make the presentation more effective and attractive** by breaking up long pieces of text.

Headings are **useful for your readers**. They explain the structure of your document and enable the reader to find a particular topic easily.

It is best to **start with headings and then write your text**. If you do it like this, your essay will be better organised than if you simply write it and try to add headings afterwards.

You can use **different levels of heading**. The lower levels are called subheadings. In a long document, main headings mark the major sections and subheadings then divide these sections.

Try not to use too many headings. As a general rule, 2 or 3 headings per A4 page would be enough. Sometimes you cannot avoid having a very short section under a heading – there may simply be very little to say about that particular point. That is fine, but try not to break up the text too much.

Key point to remember
Start with your headings, then write your text.

If you are using subheadings, it is even more important to plan your heading structure before you write, so that you have a consistent framework for the whole document. Sections of similar importance should have the same level of heading.

It is usually a good idea to number headings, especially if you want to make a table of contents. It is up to you how you number them, but a common way would be to use a system of numbers and points:

1. Main heading
1.1 subheading
1.1.1 sub-subheading

Once you have decided on a structure, you need to choose a style for your headings. Make sure the style is the same throughout the whole document.

You will need to think about the following:

- The **font type and font size** for each level of heading
- Are your headings **numbered**, and if so how?
- Are your headings **bold**, *italic*, <u>underlined</u>, etc.?
- Do they start with a **capital letter**?
- Do they include **punctuation**?
- How much **space** is there before and after the surrounding text?

Tip for success
Computer programs like Word® have headings that you can use. You can change the style if you want, then you can simply choose the heading type when you need it.

Try to make your headings as specific as possible. Instead of the heading 'Background', for example, try to express what sort of background information you are giving in this section. Make sure that your headings do accurately describe the information they include.

Try to think about your headings from the point of view of the reader and the purpose of your document.

For instance, if you are writing an explanation of how to do something, headings with verbs can be effective, e.g.:

- **Planning your vegetable garden**
- **Deciding what to grow**
- **Preparing your soil**

Sometimes it is appropriate to use questions as headings, e.g.

- **What is a carbon footprint?**
- **How can I reduce my carbon footprint?**

The reader should be able to read the text separately from the headings. Do not use pronouns in the first sentence that refer back to the heading. For example, if your heading is 'Principles of the carbon cycle', do not begin the next sentence 'This is the process ...'.

Tip for success
Before you print your document, check that there are no headings on their own at the bottom of pages.

Paragraphs

In a long piece of writing, such as an essay or a report, each paragraph should contain one separate point or idea.

The **first sentence** of each paragraph should usually introduce what the paragraph is about:

- *Smith's views have, however, been challenged by several experts.* (continue by explaining what the experts say)
- *This new law gave greater protection to workers.* (continue by describing why it did so)

Here are some useful phrases to link your paragraphs:

- ***As a result of** this research, scientists have decided ...*
- ***Meanwhile**, my brothers had been busy ...*
- ***Despite** these problems, they carried on trying to ...*
- ***Nevertheless**, she was forced to ...*
- ***However**, we did not allow ourselves to ...*
- ***On the other hand**, many people say that ...*
- ***In addition to** this work on dolphins, he ...*

Tip for success
Try not to make your paragraphs too long. If they are very long, you will probably find that they can be divided into separate points.

Style

What is good style?

When people write with good style, their writing is clear, interesting, elegant and appropriate for their audience.

The best style to use will vary according to the type of document you are writing: the kind of original, descriptive writing you would use for a piece of creative writing would not be appropriate for a factual report.

There are many aspects to writing with good style, which are discussed in this section.

However, one simple rule applies to all your work:

Avoid repeating words.

Whatever you are writing, it will sound dull and clumsy if you use the same words over and over again. If you read your work aloud, you will notice when you have done this.

Too much repetition	***Better ...***
Team A discovered ..., Team B discovered ..., Team C discovered ...	*Team A discovered ..., Team B found ..., Team C's results showed ...*

Sometimes the easiest way to avoid repetition is simply to replace one of the words with a pronoun:

Too much repetition	***Better ...***
We intend to invite all our friends and ask each friend to bring some food.	*We intend to invite all our friends and ask each of them to bring some food.*

Writing in sentences

Sentences are the building blocks of our texts. The length of your sentences will depend on who you are writing for, but very long sentences can be confusing, while very short sentences can sound childish. If your sentence is longer than about 15-20 words, see if you can divide it.

The basic rule is that each sentence should have a **verb and a subject**:

> *The vase smashed on the floor.* (vase = subject, smashed = verb)
> *My Mum plays the violin.* (My Mum = subject, plays = verb)

It is best to **avoid starting a sentence with a conjunction** such as 'and', 'but' or 'or', especially in formal writing.

Some people think it is bad style to end a sentence with a preposition such as 'on', 'up' or 'in'. However, avoiding this can sometimes lead to a rather formal style. Compare the following:

> *We were shocked to see the conditions they live in.*
> *We were shocked to see the conditions in which they live.*

As always, think about the purpose of your document and the reader to help you choose the appropriate style and tone.

> **Tip for success**
> Try reading your work aloud. If your sentences work well, it will be easy to read. See where you make natural pauses, and think about whether you need to add commas.

Do not try to run lots of sentence parts together using commas. This is a common mistake, and can be confusing.

Look at the following:

> *First we went to the Tower of London, which was fantastic, our tour guide was excellent, and we saw the crown jewels, later we had our picnic on a lawn near the ravens.*

This sentence would be much better using dashes and splitting it into separate sentences, like this:

> *First we went to the Tower of London, which was fantastic – our tour guide was excellent. We saw the crown jewels, and later we had our picnic on a lawn near the ravens.*

However, make sure you use commas where they are needed, as they can help the reader understand your sentences better.

For instance, they are needed if a subordinate clause (less important part of a sentence) comes before the main clause, e.g.:

> *If the train is late, call me from the station.*

They are also needed for adding small pieces of information about someone or something in your sentence, e.g.:

> *My sister, who is a vet, has three children.*

Tip for success
Take care with punctuation. There is a detailed explanation of how to use commas and other punctuation marks in the punctuation section of this book.

Using plain English

It is important to write in plain English. Plain English is easier to write, and certainly easier to understand. This does not mean that you need to write in baby-talk, but try to follow these rules:

- **Avoid unnecessary jargon**. Don't talk about 'interfacing' with someone when you mean 'communicating' with them, or simply 'talking' to them. Don't say 'design solution' – it's just a design.

Of course, there are times when technical and specialist terms *are* appropriate. If you are writing a science essay, you must use the correct terminology. As always, think of your reader.

- **Avoid unnecessary formality**. Ask yourself if there is a simpler word or phrase that would be appropriate for your reader.

very formal	*simpler ...*
prior to *in excess of* *in the vicinity of*	*before* *more than* *near*

- **Try to use active verbs instead of nouns**. This will make your sentences sound less complex and formal.

noun form	*active verb form*
give encouragement to *ensure the completion of* *make provision for*	*encourage* *complete* *provide*

Active or passive verbs?

It is usually better to use active verbs in your writing because the structure is simpler. Passives can sound rather formal. Compare these two sentences, for example:

> *New recycling methods have been introduced by the council.* (passive)
> *The council has introduced new recycling methods.* (active)

However, the passive can be useful in certain cases. For instance, you may use the passive if you do not want to appear to be blaming someone or criticizing someone:

> *You have not paid the money.* (active and accusing)
> *The money has not been paid.* (passive and more neutral)

You may also want to use the passive if you do not want your reader to blame you:

> *I'm sorry to report that I have lost your documents.* (active and admitting fault)
> *I'm sorry to report that your documents have been lost.* (passive and implying that it may have been someone else's fault)

The passive is also used when you do not know who carried out an action or it is irrelevant who carried out the action. This will often happen in academic writing in which the slightly more formal style is appropriate:

> *The results were analyzed in the laboratory.*
> *The buildings were knocked down in 1989.*

Avoiding clichés

A cliché is a word or phrase that has been used too often. If you use clichés, your writing will be boring. When readers see them, they may lose interest and miss your main message. They may think that if your writing is not original, your ideas cannot be original either.

You may find that clichés slip into the first draft of your writing – after all, it is because they are so well-known and come so easily to mind that they have become clichés. Read through your document and try to identify any phrases that seem to fit into this category. If English is not your first language, it may be difficult to do this. In this case, it may be a good idea to ask a native English speaker for advice.

Then ask yourself: what does this phrase actually mean? It may not really have much meaning at all, in which case you can probably delete it. Examples of this sort of cliché are:

at the end of the day
at this moment in time
with all due respect

Or it may be that the phrase has been used so much that it has lost all its power, and may well annoy your reader. Examples of this sort of cliché are:

moving the goalposts
reinvent the wheel
the best thing since sliced bread

Sometimes a simple **combination of adjective and noun** can be so overused that it becomes a cliché, e.g.:

roaring fire
vice-like grip
long-lost friend

This does not mean that such combinations should never be used, but try not to use too many obvious combinations, and choose something more original if you can.

One area of language where it is very easy to fall into the trap of using a cliché is the **simile**.

Look at the following similes:

as cold as ice
as fresh as a daisy

They are so overused that they are not powerful descriptions. Now look at the following similes, all found in real writing:

as cold as a Siberian winter
as cold as a statue of stone
as fresh as green shoots in the morning
as fresh as a big green shiny cucumber

Of course, imaginative similes like these are not suitable for all types of writing. In formal writing, it is probably best to avoid similes altogether. In more creative writing, you should aim to be descriptive and original, but your similes should fit into the overall style of the text.

Avoiding redundancy (unnecessary words)

It is very easy to use more words than you need, but too many words will make your writing less effective and may annoy your readers.

Compare the following:

> *Jack and I are of the same opinion on this matter.*
> *Jack and I agree.*
>
> *Due to the fact that the train was delayed, we were late for the concert.*
> *We were late for the concert because the train was delayed.*

Avoid 'empty' words and phrases that do not add meaning to your sentences, e.g. *in terms of*, *the fact of the matter*.

Avoid saying the same things twice. This is known as **tautology**. Consider the following:

9 a.m. in the morning	a.m. means 'in the morning' – choose one or the other
re-examine again	just say 're-examine' – the 'again' is expressed in the prefix 're-'
my personal opinion	if it's your opinion, it's personal – you don't need to say so
mutual cooperation	you can't cooperate on your own, so it must be mutual

Avoid adding illogical extra words. Consider the following:

in actual fact	if it is a fact, it must be 'actual' – just say 'in fact'
very unique	something unique is the *only* one of its kind – there are no degrees of uniqueness
added bonus	a bonus is something that you get in addition to something else – there is no need to also say 'added'

Avoiding ambiguity

Ambiguity is when something could possibly be understood in more than one way. It is an easy trap to fall into because *you* know what you mean when you write, but try to put yourself in the reader's place and make sure there is no room for doubt.

Be careful with **words that have more than one meaning**. Often the context will be enough to make it clear which meaning is intended. If you write that you are going to the bank, nobody is likely to think you are going to a river bank. However, consider the following:

> *My teacher is really funny.*
> (Is the teacher humorous or strange?)
>
> *The food was very hot.*
> (Was it a high temperature, or was it spicy?)

Make it clear whether you are using words and phrases in a **literal or figurative** sense:

> *He was in debt to his friend.*
> (Did he owe his friend money or simply feel grateful?)
>
> *There was a chasm between us.*
> (Was there a hole in the ground, or a big difference of opinion?)

Use pronouns carefully to make sure it is clear who or what they refer to:

> *Rosie had an argument with Sarah, and she started crying.*
> (Who cried, Rosie or Sarah?)

I couldn't attach the bird boxes to the posts in the garden because they weren't strong enough.
(Was it the posts or the bird boxes that weren't strong?)

Check the structure of your sentence to make sure it is clear how the parts relate to each other. Compare the following:

We talked about bullying at work.
(Ambiguous – were we at work or not?)

We talked about the issue of workplace bullying.
At work, we talked about bullying.

They told us about the murder at 11 o'clock.
(Ambiguous – did the murder happen at 11 o'clock?)

At 11 o'clock, they told us about the murder.
They told us about the murder that occurred at 11 o'clock.

Make sure it is clear what your adjectives are describing:

a large woman's handbag
(Is it the woman or the handbag that is large?)

a formal English test
(Is the test formal, or is it a test of formal English?)

Be clear about the purpose of your writing. Imagine you are a member of staff receiving a memo from your boss that includes the following:

It would be a good idea for all staff to take at least 30 minutes break for lunch.

It would not be clear whether your boss is saying that you *must* take a 30 minute break or simply that it would be a nice thing if possible.

Register

The word register refers to aspects of language such as how formal or informal it is. Compare the following:

> *They furnished us with the requisite implements.* (very formal)
> *They gave us the necessary tools.* (neutral)
> *They let us have the gear we needed.* (informal)

You should match the register of your language to the type of writing you are doing. Using the wrong register can make your writing sound odd and can even cause offence.

Register can often be shown by the choice of words or phrases:

formal	***neutral***	***informal***
wax lyrical	*speak enthusiastically*	*go on about*
of one's own volition	*voluntarily*	*off your own bat*
in the ascendancy	*becoming successful*	*on the up*

Dictionaries mark words which are formal or informal, so you can check if you are not sure. Many idioms and phrasal verbs are either informal or slightly informal, so take care to use them appropriately.

Informal language is fine for personal letters, emails, texts, etc., but for most forms of writing, a neutral or slightly formal style is more appropriate. Remember, though, that formal does not mean pompous. Do not use very formal language to try to impress – it is more important to put your ideas over clearly.

> **Tip for success**
> Do not use different registers within the same piece of writing.

Sometimes words and phrases with a particular register are needed for specific types of writing. For instance, **legal documents** often contain extremely formal language, such as '*hereunder*' or Latin words such as '*ex gratia*', which would be out of place in most other types of writing.

Similarly, some types of writing need to use very specific **technical terms**. For example, a document for medical professionals might use a word such as '*suprarenal*' instead of saying '*above the kidneys*' because this word will be understood by its readers. In scientific documents, the use of technical terms can be necessary to avoid any ambiguity.

At the other end of the scale, **literary or poetic language** such as '*lovelorn*', '*flaxen*' or '*the gloaming*' may be appropriate in some types of creative writing.

Your choice of **grammar** and the way you **structure** your sentences can also affect register. Compare the following:

The man to whom I gave my ticket.
The man I gave my ticket to.

In the first sentence, the use of 'whom' gives a formal feel to the sentence. In the second sentence, the preposition is used at the end. In the past this was considered incorrect, but it is now widely accepted, and would be appropriate for any but the most formal of documents.

It is not usually considered appropriate to use contractions (e.g. don't, he'd, wouldn't) in formal writing because they make the text sound informal.

Tone

The tone of your writing expresses your **attitude** towards the reader, and it is important that you are careful about this.

For instance, if you are writing to complain about a product or service, you need to come across as being assertive and clear about your facts. You must decide for yourself whether you want to be rude or threatening too – but if you are, make sure it is on purpose and not because you have chosen your words badly!

It can be useful to **imagine that you are talking to your reader**. What sort of tone do you want to take? For example, you might be:

chatty	authoritative	sincere	sympathetic
grateful	serious	assertive	humorous
persuasive	practical	unfriendly	offended
efficient	angry		

If you **think about what you want to achieve** with your writing, it will help you decide what tone to take. For example, if you are writing a letter to accept a job, you will probably want your tone to be friendly yet professional and show that you are pleased to have been chosen.

It is important to use language that is the **right level of difficulty** for your reader. If you use difficult words, you may sound as if you are showing off, but if you use very simple language, your reader might feel you are being patronizing.

An important issue that influences tone is the **relationship of the writer to the reader**. For instance, a suggestion for changes to working practices might have a very different tone coming from a junior employee than if it comes from a senior manager.

You should always take into account **how well you know the person** who will read your document. If you do not know them at all, you must be aware that they may be offended by a tone that is too familiar, for instance by being too informal, or by expressing views that they may not share. Humour can also be difficult – if your readers do not know you, they may be unsure whether you are joking or not.

Compare the following letters:

Dear Emma
Tom told me you broke your leg skiing – after I'd stopped laughing, it occurred to me that you must be a bit fed up, so I'm sending you these chocolates to cheer you up. See you when (if???) you can walk again,
Lizzie, x

Dear Emma
I'm so sorry to hear about your skiing accident. Your mother told me you are likely to be in plaster for some weeks, and I know how hard that will be for you. Do take good care of yourself, and I hope to hear some better news of you soon,
with love from
Aunty Bea

In the first letter, the tone is chatty and humorous, and while it might make Emma smile, if her injury is serious she might be offended that her friend is joking about it. However, if Lizzie is a very close friend, she will probably have judged the tone of the note appropriately. The second letter is much more sincere and serious and the tone shows that the writer is really concerned about Emma.

If you are angry about something, it can be very easy to let it show, sometimes without intending to. For example, look at this email:

> *Thanks for your offer of database training, but I really don't feel it's necessary, and I wouldn't want to distract you from your work, which is already behind schedule.*

The tone of the email makes it clear that the writer was offended by the offer of help and takes revenge by implying that the person offering help cannot manage their own work.

This may be what the writer intends, but if they would prefer to keep a good relationship with their colleague, something like the following would be better:

> *Thanks for the offer of database training, but I think I've managed to get to grips with it now, and I wouldn't want to take up your time unnecessarily as I know you are very busy.*

> **Key point to remember**
> The tone you choose is up to you, but if your writing does express your attitudes, make sure this is what you intended.

Emphasis

We use emphasis to draw a reader's attention to the points which are most important. There are several ways of doing this:

- **Order within the document**. It is usual to start with the most important points.

- **Order within a sentence or paragraph**. The first part of the sentence will be seen as the most important. Compare the following:

  A thorough safety assessment is needed urgently, following a number of accidents on the site.
  Following a number of accidents on the site, a thorough safety assessment is needed urgently.

In the first example, the fact that the safety assessment is needed is emphasized by coming first in the sentence. In the second example, the fact that there have been some accidents comes across as the more important point.

- **A summary of main points**. This can be done either at the beginning or the end of a document, and could take the form of ordinary text or a list. For example, a detailed report might start with a section on 'key findings' or 'key recommendations' – simply a list of the main points the author wishes to make.

- **Amount of text**. The more important a point, the more space you are likely to use discussing it. If you add too much detail about minor points, readers may be confused about what is most important.

- **Blank space around a key phrase or sentence**. This is a rather dramatic way of emphasizing one key point:

  The evidence led to one clear conclusion:
  He did not kill his wife.

- **Typeface**. It is very simple to highlight words and phrases by using different forms of typefaces such as **bold**, *italics* or underlining. Italics are probably the most commonly used:

  Please note that pupils should not bring mobile phones to school *at any time*.
  Make sure you take *all* your belongings with you.

Fonts can also be made larger or smaller for emphasis, or a different colour may be used to make certain parts of a document stand out.

- **Repetition**. Repetition can be used in several ways to emphasize points. You could make a point and then repeat it immediately, using phrases such as:

  In other words ...
  Put more simply ...

This is a useful way to stress the point you are making and also to explain it in a different way so that you can be certain that your readers will understand it.

If you are writing a long document, you may want to repeat certain points throughout it, using phrases such as:

This demonstrates yet again ...
Again we see ...

Repetition can also be a useful stylistic advice, in writing as well as in speech. You might repeat a word, a phrase or part of a phrase:

They said local businesses would close – not true. They claimed jobs would be lost – not true. They claimed traffic would increase – not true.

- **Headings**. Headings can be used to reinforce the main point that will be made in the parts they refer to.

- **Sudden change of style**. If readers are surprised by a sudden change of style, they may pay more attention to what is being said. One example would be to use a very short, snappy sentence after one or more longer, more flowing sentences:

  Architects and engineers had assured officials and residents that the techniques used in constructing the bridge would ensure that it remained solid during an earthquake. It did not.

- **Emphatic words and phrases**. These can highlight the most important points, e.g.:

  Our priority now is ...
  The crucial advantage that this scheme offers is ...

In a similar way, sentence adverbs such as 'crucially' or 'above all' signal the importance of what follows, as do adjectives such as 'urgent', 'vital' or 'essential'.

- **Punctuation**. The most obvious way to emphasize a sentence is to end it with an exclamation mark:

  We won over a thousand pounds!

Be careful with exclamation marks, though. It is fine to use them in informal letters, emails, etc, but do not use them too often. It is not usually appropriate to use them in more formal writing.

Structuring a sentence with a dash or a colon can also emphasize part of it. See, for example, how the second of these two sentences has more emphasis:

Critics described his performance as terrible.
Critics had one word for his performance: terrible.

Avoiding offence

The simple rule for avoiding offence is this:

Treat everyone equally in your writing, regardless of age, sex, race, sexual orientation or physical difference.

Always make sure that you are **aware of current customs and values**. For instance, do not assume that couples, even married couples, consist of a man and a woman: same-sex relationships, including marriage, are legal and common in many countries.

Check that the terms you use for sensitive issues such as race and disability are the **modern**, **accepted terms**, and not old-fashioned terms that might be considered offensive.

Race and religion

It goes without saying that offensive racial or religious insults or stereotypes should never be used.

However, it can sometimes be easy to display discrimination without meaning to, simply because of our cultural background. Make sure you follow these general rules:

- **Only mention race or religion if it is relevant to your writing**. If you mention someone's race or religion, ask yourself if you would have mentioned it if it was the same as yours.

- **Make sure you use accepted modern terms**, not old-fashioned ones which many now consider offensive. For instance, a term such as *Red Indian* belongs only in cowboy movies – for all other writing, use *American Indian*. Similarly, the term *African-American* is the preferred description for black Americans of African origin, not *Negro*.

- **Be aware of different cultures**. For instance, don't assume that everyone celebrates Christmas, or that July and August are always the hottest months of the year.

When writing about people whose parents or ancestors are from different races, a common and widely-accepted term is *mixed-race*. *Dual-heritage*, with its more positive connotations, is also becoming widely used. If you are in doubt about any terms connected with race or religion, check a good dictionary.

Sexism

Here are some rules for avoiding sexism in your writing:

- **Use job titles that refer to both men and women**. For example, use *police officer* rather than *policeman*; *chair* or *chairperson* instead of *chairman*.

- **Avoid the suffix -ess on jobs**. Words like *authoress* and *poetess* are very old-fashioned and patronizing, and should not be used. It is best to avoid the *-ess* suffix for jobs altogether: while the word *actress* is still used, many women in the profession prefer *actor*.

- **Do not mention a person's sex if it is not relevant**. It is usually best to avoid terms such as *male nurse* or *lady solicitor*.

- **Do not make assumptions about the sex of people in a particular profession**. Do not write things like '*businessmen and their wives*'.

- **Avoid stereotypes of roles and characteristics**. It's not necessarily Mum who cooks the dinner and Dad who fixes the car.

- **Avoid using masculine pronouns**. Sentences such as '*Each traveller must present his documents*' sound old-fashioned and sexist. Most people now consider it acceptable to use the pronoun *their* in such cases.

- **If you write to someone whose sex you do not know, do not begin your letter *Dear Sir/s***. You could use *Dear Sir/Madam* in very formal situations, or choose another form of address altogether, e.g. *Dear Friends/Dear Supporters*.

Disability

When writing about illness and disability, there are several points to bear in mind:

- **Be sure to use current, accepted terms**. Use *bipolar disorder* rather than *manic depression*, for example.

- **Do not describe someone only by their illness**. Remember that they are a person first of all, so say *someone with epilepsy* rather than *an epileptic*.

- **Try not to portray someone with a disability as a victim**. Avoid words like *victim*, *afflicted with*, *suffering from*. Say *a wheelchair user* rather than *wheelchair-bound*.

- **Do not refer to people without a disability as *normal***. Say *nondisabled* or *able-bodied* instead.

Increasing your vocabulary

The best way to increase your vocabulary is to **read a lot**. As you read, notice the words that are being used.

If you find a word you do not know, you will sometimes be able to get a good idea of its meaning from the other words around it. If not, **look it up in a dictionary**. It is not always a good idea to look up every new word as you find it, because it can be distracting, but you could **underline or highlight** some of the words and look them up at the end.

It can be useful to **keep a vocabulary notebook**, to record new words you have learned. You can arrange the words in whatever way is best for you: by alphabetical order or by subject.

Try to develop an interest in words, and ask yourself questions about them. For instance, you can widen your vocabulary by learning **words in groups**. If you know that *canine* means 'referring to dogs', see if you know the word meaning 'relating to cats' (*feline*) or 'relating to cows' (*bovine*). Similarly, if you know that *carnivorous* means 'meat-eating', do you know the word for 'plant-eating' (*herbivorous*) or for creatures that eat anything (*omnivorous*)?

Notice the context that words are in. You can often make your writing more elegant by choosing which words go together, such as the interesting verbs with the common nouns in these examples:

> ***abandon*** *an attempt*
> ***draw*** *to a close*
> ***adopt*** *a method*

Word games such as **crossword puzzles** can help to develop an interest in words and can introduce words you did not know before.

Using a thesaurus

Look at very common words in your writing and see if there are any more interesting or specific words you could use instead. You could use a thesaurus for this. A thesaurus is a reference book which shows lists of words with similar meanings. Some word processing systems have a thesaurus built into them, so that you can click on a word for suggestions of different words with similar meanings:

if you have written ...	***consider whether you could use ...***
difficult	*ambitious, demanding, gruelling, knotty, laborious*
eat	*bolt, consume, gulp, sample, wolf down*
boring	*bland, characterless, dreary, insipid, soul-destroying*

Using a dictionary

A good dictionary will help a lot with your writing. Try to use a dictionary that is **suitable for you**. For instance, if you are at school, a special **schools dictionary** should have all the words you need for all your subjects, but not be too big to carry around. If English is not your first language, try to use a **learner's** dictionary, which will have simple definitions, lots of example sentences, and all the grammar information you need.

Digital dictionaries

There are many types of digital dictionary available now. Tiny **handheld** ones are easy to carry around, and online dictionaries and dictionary apps can be used from your computer, tablet, smartphone, etc.

A lot of book dictionaries come with either a **CD-ROM** or with a code that gives you access to an **online dictionary**. There are many free online dictionaries also available. Try to choose one that comes from a good publisher and that is suitable for your needs.

CD-ROM and Internet dictionaries can be extremely useful because they can do things that are impossible in paper books. For instance, if you don't know how to spell a word, you can just type in the letters you are sure of, and all the words containing those letters will be found. Many of these dictionaries have extra information such as synonyms and antonyms, the ability to search for vocabulary in topics, and extra examples. You can also hear spoken pronunciations, rather than trying to work them out from symbols.

Information in dictionaries

Dictionaries are not just for meanings and spelling, although of course these are very important uses. Dictionaries can give you information on:

- **Irregular inflections**. If words do not have regular patterns, this will be shown. For instance, you can see that the plural of *genus* is *genera* or that the past participle of *sink* is *sunk*.
- **Variant spellings**. You can see which words have more than one spelling, eg. *caftan* and *kaftan*.
- **Regional information**. You can see when words and spelling are used in a particular variety of English, e.g. *courgette* is used in British English, but Americans say *zucchini* for the same vegetable.
- **Example sentences**. Many dictionaries give example sentences, showing how to use a word in context.
- **Etymology**. Large dictionaries often give information about the origins of words and phrases.
- **Register**. A dictionary will tell you if a word is formal, informal, etc.
- **Pronunciation**. This is usually shown using a set of symbols.

Terms used in writing English

The following are important terms that refer to different styles of writing and types of words and phrases. You need to know them for studying literature, and also to be aware of them for using in your own writing.

Antonyms

An antonym is a word with an opposite meaning. *Legal* and *illegal* are antonyms, as are *mature* and *immature*.

Alliteration

Alliteration is the use of the same letter or sound (especially consonants) at the beginning of two or more words that are close together in a sentence:

> *droplets of dew at dawn*

Assonance

Assonance is the repetition of vowel sounds in two or more words that are close together in a sentence:

> *I laughed, but my heart was torn apart.*

Euphemism

A euphemism is a word or phrase that is used to avoid talking directly about something that is embarrassing, upsetting or offensive.

Euphemisms can be used in personal writing to show tact to your reader. For instance, in a letter of sympathy, some people prefer to use the euphemism *passed away* rather than *died*. Euphemisms can be used to avoid embarrassment to readers who are uncomfortable with words connected with sex or bodily functions.

Euphemisms are sometimes used in quite formal writing in order deliberately to disguise an unpleasant truth. For instance, a company press release might talk about *restructuring* or *rationalizing* rather than *sacking staff*. In war, the terms *collateral damage* or *friendly fire* sound much less terrible than the reality of what they describe.

There is no place for euphemism in scientific or technical writing.

Figurative language

Figurative language is where an extra, more imaginative meaning comes from a literal meaning. For instance, the literal meaning of the word *chasm* is 'a large hole in the ground', whereas the figurative meaning refers to a fundamental difference of opinion between people.

Idioms

Idioms are phrases such as *give someone a hand* and *be over the moon*, where the meaning is not the same as the literal meaning of all the words in the phrase.

Metaphor

Metaphor is the use of a particular word or phrase – usually a concrete noun - to describe the characteristics of something else. For instance we might say *She has a heart of ice*, meaning that she shows no sympathy or emotion.

Proverbs

Proverbs are short sentences that many people know, often expressing advice, or something that many people believe to be true. Examples of proverbs are *Marry in haste, repent at leisure* and *Spare the rod and spoil the child*.

Similes

Similes are phrases such *as as dull as ditchwater* or *sing like an angel*, which compare one thing to another. The difference between a simile and a metaphor is that similes say that something is *like* something else, whereas a metaphor says something *is* something else.

Synonyms

Synonyms are words with the same or similar meanings. For instance, *clever* is a synonym of *intelligent*. However, it is important to note that words with similar meanings often have subtle differences in register or tone. *Purchase* is more formal than *buy*, for instance, while *slim* is a much more positive description than *skinny*.

Special information

Speech

There are two ways of writing about what someone said:

- In **direct speech**, we repeat the actual words used:

  'There is nothing we can do about it,' Mona said.

- In **reported speech** (also called **indirect speech**), we make the words part of our own sentence, usually using a verb such as 'say', 'announce' or 'explain':

  Mona said that there was nothing we could do about it.

Direct speech

Direct speech is common in novels and other writing where the actual words of speakers are quoted. The reporting verb (e.g. *say*, *announce*, *explain*) may come before the words that were spoken, or after them, or at a natural pause inside the reported sentence:

> ***Mona said**, 'There is nothing we can do about it.'*
> *'There is nothing we can do about it,' **Mona said**.*
> *'It's no good,' **Mona said**, 'We'll just have to ask for help.'*

The words spoken must be written inside inverted commas. They can be single (' ') or double (" "). In American English, double quotation marks are usually used.

The words spoken always begin with a capital letter as long as the sentence is not divided by a reporting verb. The comma comes inside the inverted commas unless the sentence is divided by a reporting verb:

> *'**G**ive her a chance,' Jamie begged.*
> *'**T**here is', Mona said, 'nothing we can do about it.'*

If the words spoken are a question or an exclamation, there is no comma but a question mark or an exclamation mark, which comes inside the inverted commas:

> *'Why did you do it**?**' she asked.*
> *'Oh, mind your own business**!**' he snapped.*

The subject and reporting verb can be used either way round:

> *'There is nothing we can do about it,' **Mona said**.*
> *'There is nothing we can do about it,' **said Mona**.*

> **Tip for success**
> If you are writing a long stretch of direct speech between two characters, it is not always necessary to use reporting verbs each time. As long as it is clear which character is speaking, you can just start a new line within new inverted commas each time a different character speaks.

Reported speech

When you use reported speech, the words put into the reported clause do not exactly match the words actually spoken. For example, you will need to change pronouns, words like *here* and *there*, or the tense of the sentence:

> *I believe **you**.*
> *She said that she believed **us**.*
> *I've been **here** before.*
> *He said that he had been **there** before.*
> ***I've done** the housework.*
> *He said **he had done** the housework.*

Reported speech always has two clauses: the **reported clause** which contains the words that were spoken, usually in a slightly different form, and the **main clause** which contains the reporting verb.

The main clause usually comes first:

> ***Katie told me*** *that Marie is going to resign.*
> ***Sara asked*** *whether Hardeep was feeling better.*

If the main reported clause is a statement, the main clause is linked to the reported clause by *that*:

> *Monique said* ***that*** *her favourite actor was Ben Whishaw.*
> *John replied* ***that*** *he preferred Scarlett Johansson.*

The linking word *that* can be left out after most reporting verbs except those that mean 'answer':

> *She told me* ***(that)*** *she was going to leave.*
> *I replied* ***that*** *I was very sorry to hear that.*

If the main reported clause is a question, the main verb will be a question word such as *ask*, *inquire*, *wonder*, *query*. The link between the main clause will be *if* or *whether*:

> *She asked me* ***if*** *I was comfortable.*
> *He inquired* ***whether*** *the changes had been made.*

Reported clauses can also be used to express what someone is thinking as well as what is actually spoken:

> *Hussain* ***wondered*** *whether* ***the concert would be sold out****.*
> *Charlotte* ***thought*** *that* ***she had better go and see her family****.*

Key point to remember
Speech in a reported clause is not separated from the reporting verb by a comma, is not enclosed in inverted commas, and does not begin with a capital letter unless it is a proper noun. Reported questions are not followed by question marks.

Questions

There are three main ways of making questions in English:

- With a **question word**, such as *who*, *why*, *how*:

  ***Who** won the race?*
  ***Which** team was it?*

- With an **auxiliary verb** (*do*, *have* or *be*):

  ***Do** your children like sport?*
  ***Have** you seen her latest movie?*

- With a modal verb, such as *can* or *may*:

  ***Can** Mahmoud come too?*
  ***May** I see the letter?*

Occasionally, we express sentences by our tone of voice, but this would only be appropriate for written English if you are writing direct speech:

*'**She's left her job?** I thought she was happy there.'*

Negative forms of questions almost always use contractions:

***Doesn't** he like talking about his childhood?*
***Can't** Peter have one too?*

If the full *not* form is used, it comes immediately after the subject. The full form is very formal:

***Does** he **not** like talking about his childhood?*
***Can** Peter **not** have one too?*

Questions should always have a question mark at the end, even if they are headings. The only time that a question does not have a question mark is if it is written in reported speech:

> *Do you like cats?*
> *He asked me if I liked cats.*

Sentence tags

Sentence tags look like short questions and are used the end of sentences. They are sometimes called **question tags**, but many sentences ending with a tag are not real questions.

They are usually used to check that the listener or reader agrees with what the speaker or writer has said. Sentence tags are used very commonly in speech and in informal writing such as a chatty email, but rarely in formal written English.

If you need to write them, either in a piece of informal writing, or if you are quoting direct speech, remember that they have a comma before them, and a question mark at the end:

> *You've seen the programme**, haven't you?***
> *Well, we can't jump over it**, can we?***
> *You aren't listening**, are you?***

Quotations

There are many reasons to use quotations in your writing:

- To show how the **ideas and research of others** have contributed to your own work.
- To **add evidence** to your arguments, particularly from respected sources.
- To **show different opinions**, sometimes ones which disagree with yours.
- To **add interest or humour** to your writing. If someone has said something particularly clever or witty about your subject, it can liven up your text to quote it.
- In writing about literary works, to give **samples of text for analysis**.

However, do not be tempted to include too many quotations. You are the author, and your ideas and analysis are the most important part of your writing. Your writing should not rely too heavily on quotations – they should be there to support your work but not to form the main part of it.

Make sure that any quotations you do add are there for a good reason – do not put them in simply to make your document longer. Too many quotations can interrupt the flow of your writing and make the text seem cluttered.

Remember that there is a big difference between quoting and **plagiarizing**, which means using the work of others as if it were your own. Even if you use different words rather than quoting directly, if you are using someone else's ideas, you should say so.

Always make sure your quotations are **accurate**. If you have found your quotation as a quotation in someone else's work, you should go back to the original source, if possible, to check it.

It is **not necessary to use whole sentences** in quotes – in fact it is usually best to use only the parts that are relevant to your argument. However, if you take a sentence out of a paragraph, or a word or phrase out of a sentence, make sure that you do not change the author or speaker's intended meaning.

If you use a quote, you must always **explain why you have used it** and what you think its importance is. This can be done very simply. For example, if the quotation clearly backs up a point you have just made, you could use a phrase like:

> *As x says ...*

Other quotations may need more **analysis and explanation**. You cannot assume that your reader will draw the same conclusions from a quotation as you do, so you must make it very clear what you think its significance is. You might start your next sentence with phrases such as:

> *This shows that ...*
> *[The author] is clearly of the opinion that ...*
> *Put more simply, this means ...*

It is often useful to give a **context** for your quotation, for example by explaining when and where it was written or spoken, or the situation the writer or speaker was in.

How to show quotations

For long quotations (around 60 words or more), it is common to use a separate paragraph, indented slightly from the rest of the text and often using a slightly smaller font.

Shorter quotations are usually shown as part of a sentence:

> *Greenshaw argued that 'the upper classes are not capable of compassion'.*
> *She described the children as 'motivated and alert'.*

Quotations can also follow an introductory clause, using a colon or a comma before the inverted comma:

> *Charles made a pronouncement: 'There will be no more discussion on this matter.'*
> *Oscar Wilde once said, 'Always forgive your enemies; nothing annoys them so much.'*

If you are quoting lines of poetry, it is usual to show the ends of lines with /:

> *As an unperfect actor on the stage,/Who with his fear is put beside his part*

If you want to **omit part of a quotation**, you can use [...]:

> *She described the play as 'racist in a way that was typical of that time, and deeply upsetting'.*
> *She described the play as 'racist [...] and deeply upsetting'.*

If you want to add something to a quotation, you use square brackets:

> *Giving evidence, then he said, 'I went round to his house with Al [Albert Flynn, brother of the accused].'*

If a quotation contains an error, for instance of spelling or grammar, or if it contains something that is surprising, shocking or offensive, and you want to stress that this is *really* what the person said or wrote, use [*sic*], which is Latin for *thus*:

Clarke wrote that he 'could of [sic] done it'.
(This should be *'could have done it'*.)

Quoting or paraphrasing?

Sometimes you may want to use your own words to explain what someone else has said. This is called paraphrasing. There could be several reasons for this:

- The original quote might be too long, so you need to summarize.
- The original quote might be written in language that is too difficult, so you need to simplify it.
- You might not want to break up your own text with too many direct quotes.

Think about the purpose of your quotations. For example, in an essay on literature, it may be necessary to have a lot of quotations so that you can discuss and analyze the actual language of the author. For a science essay, it may be more appropriate to paraphrase most of the ideas you discuss.

If you do paraphrase, you must still make it clear whose work you are using. Make sure that your paraphrase does not change the meaning of the original in any way – if you want to add your own comments, or disagree with it, you must make it clear which are your ideas and which are the ideas of the person you are paraphrasing.

Referencing quotations

If you use a quotation, you should always say who the speaker or author is, and – if at all possible – what the source was.

This can be done **within the text**, using your own words to introduce the quotation:

As Juliet says in Shakespeare's Romeo and Juliet, 'Parting is such sweet sorrow.'
In a speech during his visit to Berlin in 1963, US President John F Kennedy famously said, 'Ich bin ein Berliner'.

In **academic writing**, it is usual to refer to a footnote or a bibliography (list of books you used) to reference a quotation. Styles for this can vary, so it a good idea to ask your teacher if there is a recommended style. A common way would be to show the author and the date of the publication in brackets in the main text, then show the whole source in the bibliography.

In the text:

As Prof Williams points out: 'There is a measurable difference between the amount people claim to eat and the amount they actually eat.' (Williams, 2007, p.25)

In the bibliography:

Williams, J. (2007) *The Causes of Obesity.* Newtown: Newtown University Press

If you use a **quotation from a website**, you must reference it in a similar way. Again, there are different styles for this, but a common way would be:

Author, A (date) *Title of article or web page.* Available at: article.com. Accessed on 17/04/2015

Proper nouns

Names of people

Names of people should always be written with capital letters:

Ivan Gorecki
Julia Jones

Titles, such as *Mr*, *Mrs*, *Ms*, *Dr* can be written with or without full stops:

Ms Hooper
Prof. McCarthy

Geographical terms

Remember to use capital letters for all of the following:

- Countries, e.g. *Japan*, *Sweden*
- Nationalities, e.g. *Japanese*, *Swedish*
- Other geographical locations, e.g. *Mount Everest*, *Lake Tahoe*
- Languages, e.g. *French*, *Swahili*

When writing geographical names that begin with *the*, it is more common to use a lower case *t*:

the United States
the Alps

Names of companies and products

Names of companies and products usually have capital letters:

Nokia
Coca Cola

Be careful to spell the name of companies and products exactly as they are spelled by their owners. For instance, the name of the publisher of this book is *HarperCollins*, with no space before the second capital letter.

In formal writing, or writing that is to be published, you need to find out if a company name or product name is a registered trademark, and if it is, to put a trademark symbol (®) after the word.

Names of books/films, etc

Capital letters are used for the first letter in titles of books, magazines, newspapers, TV shows, films, etc. Where there are several words, capitals are usually used for the main content words, unless they are the first word in the title:

> *The Wall Street Journal*
> *The Merchant of Venice*
> *Gone with the Wind*

If you mention titles such as these in your text, they should be in italic:

> He decided to write a letter to *The Times*.
> Her last book, *Diary of a Wife*, deals with the subject of domestic violence.

The exceptions to this rule are The Bible and The Koran, which remain in ordinary type.

Abbreviations

It can sometimes be difficult to decide when to use full stops in abbreviations. In British English, it is becoming more common to use abbreviations without full stops, while in American English, they are used more often. In both varieties of English, there are some forms of abbreviation where it is more common to use full stops that others.

In some cases, you may make your decision based on the need to avoid ambiguity, e.g. *a.m.* rather than am. Make sure that you treat each form consistently throughout your text.

You must be certain that your readers will understand any abbreviations you use. It is safe to use widely understood abbreviations like *VAT* or *NHS*, though even in these cases, if your audience is not British, you may need to add an explanation. However, less common abbreviations could puzzle your readers, so it is best either to avoid them, or to put the full form in brackets the first time you use them.

There are a few abbreviations which are so much more widely used than their full forms that it is not necessary to given the full forms at all. Examples are *DNA* and *TNT*.

Abbreviations formed from the first letter of all the words can be spelled with or without full stops, though it is now more common in British English to omit them:

> *BBC (British Broadcasting Company)*
> *FBI (Federal Bureau of Investigation)*

Abbreviations formed from the first part of a word are more likely to use full stops:

> *Prof. (Professor)*
> *Oct. (October)*

Abbreviations formed from the first and last letters of a word do not usually have a full stop in British English:

Mr (mister)
Dr (doctor)

Abbreviations formed from Latin words often use full stops:

e.g. (exempli gratia = for example)
i.e. (id est = that is to say)
etc. (et cetera = the other things)

However, the common Latin abbreviation *AD (anno domini = in the year of the lord)* and its earlier partner *BC (= before Christ)* are more commonly used without full stops.

Abbreviations for metric scientific measurements are often formed from the first letter of each of the parts of a compound word. They do not use full stops, and never add an *s* to form their plurals:

*kg (**k**ilo**g**ram or kilograms)*
*ml (**m**illi**l**itre or millilitres)*

Abbreviations for imperial measurements are often very irregular, and often do have full stops. Like metric abbreviations, they do not add *s* in the plural:

oz. (ounce or ounces) Comes from the Italian word *onza*
lb. (pound or pounds, in weight) Comes from the Latin word *libra*

Acronyms

Acronyms are words formed from the first letters of several words or from parts of words. The difference between acronyms and other abbreviations is that acronyms are pronounced as words themselves, rather than as individual letters:

NATO (North Atlantic Treaty Organization)
GUI (graphical user interface)

Acronyms are not usually written with full stops. In fact, many acronyms make a journey from being abbreviations to becoming words in their own right. For example, an acronym such as *AIDS (acquired immune deficiency/immunodeficiency syndrome)* has become so widely used, that it is often written *Aids*.

Other words have completed the journey – nobody really thinks of words like *laser (Light Amplification by Stimulated Emission of Radiation)* or *scuba (self contained underwater breathing apparatus)* as being abbreviations at all.

Numbers

Numbers can be written using figures or letters:

1	*one*
350	*three hundred and fifty*
1,299	*one thousand, two hundred and ninety nine*

Note that we put a comma or a space between each group of three figures, counting from the right:

3,490
2 350 100

In mathematical and scientific writing, numbers are always written as figures. In general writing, you can use words or figures:

480 coulombs is equivalent to 0.005 faradays.
About two hundred people attended the meeting.
We'll need 50 chairs.

It is quite common to use words for numbers less than 10, and figures for larger numbers. Whatever you decide, be consistent throughout your writing.

However, if you have two numbers together, you may use a combination to avoid confusion:

Three 5-year olds were hurt in a road accident near Leeds.

Very large numbers in the millions, billions or even higher are usually written like this:

40 million
3 billion

Notice that there is no s on the end of *million* and *billion*.

When there has been more than one king or queen with the same name, their name is followed by an ordinal number, usually written in roman numerals:

Henry VIII
Elizabeth II

Tip for success
Take care with spelling the number *forty* – there is no *u* in it.

Dates

There are several accepted ways of writing dates:

> *11th June* 1961
> *11 June*, 1961
> *11 June* 1961
> *11.6.61*
> *11/06/1961*

The style you choose will depend on what you are writing – the longer styles are suitable for essays, polite letters or other formal writing, while the shorter styles are used in quick emails, filling in forms, etc.

Note that in British English, we usually order dates: day – month – year. In American English, it is more common to order them: month – day – year:

> *June 11th*, 1961

If you are writing about centuries, the most common style is:

> *During the 15th century ...*

Remember that the name of the century is always the number above the beginning of the years in it, so for instance 1492 is in the 15th century, and 1997 is in the 20th century.

When we are writing about history, the abbreviations BC and AD are used for dates before and after the birth of Christ.

AH means 'year 1' in the Muslim calendar. It is the equivalent of AD 622.

> **Tip for success**
> Note that non-Christian writers often prefer to avoid the abbreviations BC and *AD* and use *BCE* *(before the common era)* and CE *(of the common era)* instead.

Foreign words and phrases

There are many words in English that come from other languages originally, but then become so absorbed into English that we do not think of them as being foreign any more. Examples are *bazaar* from Persian, *karate* from Japanese and *intelligentsia* from Russian. These words are used in just the same way as any other English words.

However, for a word or phrase that is self-consciously foreign, *italics* are often used:

> The same complaint was repeated *ad nauseam*.
> (Latin = until we were sickened)
> *Entre nous*, his finances are in a perilous state.
> (French = between ourselves)
> Her writings displayed a bleak *Weltanschauung*.
> (German = view of life and the world)

Sometimes it can be difficult to decide if a word has entered mainstream English. If you are unsure whether or not to use italics, consider whether your reader is likely to think of the word or phrase as being part of 'normal' English.

For instance, if you know a lot about yoga, terms such as *chi* (vital energy) and *chakra* (one of the points of physical or spiritual energy) will probably be well known to you. If you are writing for an audience which is also knowledgeable about yoga, you can probably use them without italics and without explanation. However, if your writing is for a general audience, it is best to use italics to indicate that these are words of foreign origin (Chinese and Sanskrit), and also to explain them, at least the first time they are used.

Many foreign words and phrases will only be suitable in very formal or intellectual forms of writing.

Checking your work

General checks

It is important to **leave time to check your work**, so that the finished quality is as high as possible. Checking falls into two main areas:

- **Overall structure and content**.

- **Detailed points of spelling, grammar, punctuation, etc**.

If you have planned your work carefully and written one or more drafts, as described in the section on 'Planning' in this book, your work should already be logical and well structured. However, even for a short piece of writing, such as a letter or work email, it is worth asking yourself the following questions:

- Has my writing achieved what I wanted to achieve?
- Have I expressed my points clearly?
- Do my ideas or pieces of information come in a logical sequence?
- Do I have enough evidence to support my points?
- Is the tone of my writing what I wanted it to be?
- Have I included everything I wanted to include?

It can often be a good idea to **ask someone else** to correct your work – your eyes will see what you *intended* to write, whereas someone else may spot errors more easily.

Tip for success
Most people find it easier to check their work on paper rather than on a computer screen, so if it is important that it is correct, consider printing it out.

Checking spelling

It is important to make sure your spelling is correct. There is a section on spelling in this book which gives general rules, and also a section on words which are often spelled wrongly.

Use your instinct: if a word looks wrong, check it in a dictionary. You can also use a spellchecker on your computer, but make sure that it is set to the variety of English you want – for example, British or American.

General points to look out for include:

- **Homophones**. These are words which sound the same but are spelled differently, e.g. their/there, witch/which, bare/bear. Remember that the spellchecker on your computer will not be able to correct errors in homophones because they are both correct words.
- **Letters that are the wrong way round**. It is very easy to make this kind of error when you are typing your work, for instance typing '*form*' instead of '*from*'.
- **Missing letters**. Make sure you do not miss out silent letters in words such as 'gover**n**ment', or forget to double the consonant in words such as 'swi**mm**ing'.

> **Tip for success**
> Take particular care with typed writing – it is much easier to make a mistake with fingers on keys than with a pen.

Checking grammar and punctuation

There are sections on grammar and punctuation in this book that give general rules, and also a section on common errors.

General points to look out for include:

- **Apostrophes**. Make sure you have put them in where they are needed and left them out where they are not.
- **Capital letters**. Make sure that all proper nouns have capital letters. It is also a common error to put a lower case 'i' where the upper case pronoun 'I' is needed.
- **Repeated words**. These are often found at the end of one line and the beginning of another.
- **Missing words**. It can be very easy to miss out little words such as 'of' or 'in', and equally difficult to spot that they are missing, since your brain can compensate by adding them in unconsciously when you read.
- **Agreement**. This means making sure that all the parts of a sentence relate correctly to each other, avoiding mistakes such as '*We was asked to contribute*.' (Should be: *We were asked to contribute*.)

If you are using your computer to write, you will probably have a grammar checker available. This will pick up some common problems, but you should still check your work yourself.

Tip for success
Do not try to correct huge pieces of text in one go – you need to be fresh to be able to spot errors.

Other things to check

- **Facts and information**. If there is any doubt about the source of your information, for instance if it came from a website you are not sure is reliable, make sure you can confirm it in another, more reliable source.

- **Numbers**. Always check numbers, especially long ones such as telephone numbers. It is very easy to make a mistake when you type these.

- **Dates**. If you tell people a meeting is on Thursday 6th, but the 6th is a Wednesday, you will cause confusion.

- **Repetition of words and phrases**. As you were writing, you may not have realised that you used the same word or phrase over and over again, but when you check at the end, you will notice this, and can vary your words if you want to.

- **References**. If you have referred to another book, paper, etc., make sure you have acknowledged it and referenced it properly. In the same way, if you have used charts, diagrams, etc,. make sure there are references to them all in the text.

- **Cross references**. If you have a long document, with many different, numbered sections, you may want to cross refer from one to another, and it is best to do this at the end, when your section headings will not change. If you are writing on a computer, you will be able to set up your document so that cross references change automatically if the heading numbers change.

Checking work written on a computer

In many ways, computers have made all sorts of writing much easier, especially because we can correct mistakes and move around sections of text without having to write everything out again. However, this does mean that it is very easy to introduce mistakes.

If you correct one word in a sentence or one part of a sentence, take great care to make sure that the whole sentence is still correct. For instance, it is very easy to leave in words that are not needed. Look at the following example:

> *She had an important role in his career.*
> *His mother played had an important role in his career.*

The writer only deleted '*she*' instead of '*she had*' when making this correction, leading to an extra verb in the sentence.

Remember, too, to make sure that agreement within a sentence is not affected by a change to part of it:

> *I gave my passport to the officer, who looked at it closely.*
> *I gave my passport and driving licence to the officer, who looked at it closely.*

In this case, the writer has added the words '*and driving licence*' but has forgotten to change the pronoun '*it*' later in the sentence to '*them*'.

> **Tip for success**
> If you decide to move a section of text, do make sure that you have deleted it from where it was originally.

Marking your corrections

It is usually best to **mark up a whole document or section of a document on paper** before you actually make the changes on the computer.

When people do **proofreading** in a formal way, there is a set of standard marks that they use. It is unlikely that you will need to learn formal proofreading marks, but some of them can be useful, as they are a clear way of showing your changes, particularly if you are **correcting someone else's writing**.

For example, the mark ^ shows *where* something is to be added, and the text in the margin shows *what* is to be added. The symbol # shows where a space should be added and the symbol ⅂ in the margin indicates that the words in the text with a line through them should be deleted.

There are several books and websites which explain how to use proofreading symbols.

If you are **correcting someone else's work on screen**, it can be useful to use a system that shows the changes you suggest, rather than simply making the changes yourself. That way, the author can decide whether to accept or reject your corrections. You can also leave explanations, comments and suggestions that the author can delete later.

Key point to remember
Printing out your work and reading through it on paper can be a helpful way of spotting mistakes.

Tip for success
If possible, ask someone else to correct your writing. Errors that you cannot spot yourself may be very obvious to a person who is looking at a piece of text for the first time.

Writing

PART TWO

Formal or work emails

Email is very much faster than writing letters. You can receive a reply to an email within seconds – or minutes – of sending one. In this way, email is more **like conversation** than paper-based writing. This is its great advantage: email communication, like conversation, can be **two-way** and **almost immediate**. It can also be its weakness when people do not take enough care writing emails, especially formal or work emails.

First, here are some general points about email to keep in mind:

- Email tends to be brief.
- Email is generally less formal than communication on paper.
- Email does not communicate emotions as successfully as speech. The reader of your email may not be able to tell from your words if you are serious or joking, angry or just surprised.
- Emails, especially very short emails, can sound angry, unfriendly or rude when this is not intended by the writer.

Key point to remember
Emails that are written very quickly and carelessly can sound unfriendly and rude.

The **rules are less strict** for writing formal or work *emails* than for writing formal *letters*. People have been writing letters for many hundreds of years so rules have had time to develop. Email, as a recent form of communication, is much less fixed in its rules.

The **rules are** also **different** in different countries and cultures and in different places of work. This point is worth remembering. What is right for one group of people may not be right for all people.

It is also true to say that **everyone** has **their own style** of writing emails. Even within the same company, two people may take very different approaches to this form of communication.

The points laid out in this unit are therefore a **guide to writing formal emails**. By following these generally accepted rules, you will get the most out of email. You will also avoid some of the most frequent problems that arise from this form of communication.

Tip for Success
When you join a new company, notice how your colleagues write their emails and consider changing your style to fit in with the company style.

Salutations for formal emails

(Words or phrases used for saying hello)

It is generally a good idea to **start an email with a greeting** rather than beginning the message immediately. Just like a face-to-face exchange of greetings, email greetings:

- show that you are friendly and pleasant
- show respect for the reader

In addition, a greeting allows the reader to pause for a moment before reading the message itself.

If, however, you and a colleague are writing a series of short emails to each other on a particular subject, the rules are different. It is generally acceptable after the first exchange of emails to include only the information, without salutations.

Note that if you are using **instant messaging**, which is an even faster method of communication, you only need to add a salutation to the first in a series of messages that you send to someone.

There are no fixed rules for the type of greeting that you use. Generally, if you are emailing someone that you work with or even someone that you do not know, it is acceptable to **start the email** with a simple '**Hello**' or '**Hello James**'. (If you know the colleague well, '**Hi**' or '**Hi James**' might also be fine.)

You may want to **show more respect** in your greeting, perhaps if the person is much older than you, has a higher rank than you in the same company, or is from a country or culture that is more formal than yours. If you are in any doubt about this, you could address the person, '**Dear Mr Sanchez**' or '**Dear Ms Sanchez**'.

If you are replying to an email and the sender of the message has used his or her first name only, it is generally **acceptable to use their first name** too.

Key point to remember
If you decide to use the more formal salutation 'Dear Mr Sanchez' or 'Dear Ms Sanchez' make sure that you use the correct title. If the person you are emailing is a doctor, for example, be sure to include that in the salutation.

Subject lines

People who use email for work often complain that they receive too much email and that it takes up too much of their time dealing with it.

You can help with this situation by **making full use of the subject line**. The subject line gives you the chance to tell the reader of your email **why you are emailing them** before they have even opened your message.

For example, if you are emailing a company to ask for information about a product, in the subject line, write the name of the product and the fact that you need information:

Subject: Balance bike (ref: N765) info required

The subject line gives you the chance to **show the main points** of your email. If you start to type 'Hi' or 'Another thing' in the subject line, think for a moment whether you can replace it with something more useful.

Look at the following subject lines and see how, in only a few words, you can show the main points of an email:

Subject: Meeting Room changed to mr5

Subject: Lunch (Fri 9 Oct) cancelled

Subject: REQ: Jan's sales figures

Subject: Reminder: 5-year plan due

Tip for Success
Write a useful subject line that says in just a few words what your email is about and what, if any, action you need the reader to take.

Content and length

Before you even start to type your message, make sure you can answer the following two questions:

- Why am I writing this?
- What do I want the reader of this email to do?

Remember that most people receive a lot of email in the course of a working day. For this reason, they do not welcome long emails! Your job is therefore to **tell them your point or points quickly and clearly**. Here are a few tips to help you do this:

- Make the first sentence count. Introduce the topic of the email clearly and in a few words.
- Write in short paragraphs. Separate paragraphs, each relating to a different point, will make the information easier to understand. Do not allow important points to get lost in one long paragraph.
- Consider using headings within the body of your message if the message relates to several different subjects.
- Consider numbering your points. The reader will find this useful when responding to particular points.
- Leave a space between each paragraph.
- Use short sentences. Try to keep your sentences to a maximum of 20 words. These can be quickly read and understood.
- If possible, try to fit your message onto one screen so that the reader does not have to scroll down to see the rest of it.

Read the following email. Consider:

- Is the information presented in the clearest way?
- Did the writer think about the needs of the reader as she wrote her email?

Subject: conference dinner
From: "Hill, Lucy" <Lucy.Hill@bigbooks.co.uk>
To: "Ollie Walsh"

Hi Ollie

Thanks again for offering to help out with the arrangements for the conference dinner. I do appreciate it. I met with David yesterday to finalize details and here's what we decided: The venue (Carmichael Hall) is booked for Dec 18th, 7:00 – 12:00. Your contact there is Julia Winters on 01354 638976. Invitations should go out to all conference delegates the week starting November 3rd. The invitations are currently with the printers, btw, and when they are returned to us (this Friday) will need checking against the original delegate list which I'll get Sujata to send to you. Hallidays, the caterers, will need to know final numbers by Dec. 10th, latest. Please call them to let them know. Last of all, please could you liaise with Sujata over the timing of the speeches and let the relevant people know when their slot is.

Many thanks,
Lucy

Now see how much clearer the same message looks when the writer considers what will be most helpful to the reader and has:

- broken the text up into separate, short paragraphs
- given each paragraph a heading
- allowed plenty of white space

Subject: conference dinner
From: "Hill, Lucy" <Lucy.Hill@bigbooks.co.uk>
To: "Ollie Walsh"

Hi Ollie

Thanks again for offering to help out with the arrangements for the conference dinner. I do appreciate it. I met with David yesterday to finalize details and here's what we decided:

Venue
The venue (Carmichael Hall) is booked for Dec 18th, 7:00 – 12:00. Your contact there is Julia Winters on 01354 638976

Invitations
The invitations are currently with the printers. When they are returned to us (this Friday) they will need checking against the original delegate list which I'll get Sujata to send to you. Invitations should go out to all conference delegates the week starting November 3rd.

The caterers
Hallidays, the caterers, will need to know final numbers by Dec. 10th. Please call them to let them know.

Speeches
Last of all, please could you liaise with Sujata over the timing of the speeches and let the relevant people know when their slot is.

Many thanks,
Lucy

Tone

Read the following email and ask yourself how the writer was feeling when he wrote it:

Subject: conference dinner
From: "Walsh, Ollie" <Ollie.Walsh@bigbooks.co.uk>
To: "Lucy Hill"

Lucy,

There are problems re the arrangements for the conference dinner:

1. The invitations have only just arrived this morning so I will be late sending them out.

2. Julia Winters called late yesterday. She was under the impression that 150 people were attending. Sujata's list says it's 170. Which of these is right?

3. Re the speeches, Alice and David are fine with 10 minutes each but Michael wants 15 minutes. Is he allowed 15 minutes? Also, you didn't ask Saskia to speak and she's offended. Did you mean not to ask her or is this an oversight?

Ollie

Perhaps the writer of this email was angry or stressed. That is certainly the impression that his email gives. However, it is possible that he was neither angry not stressed: he simply needed advice from Lucy about how to act. Supposing he was not angry, how might he have written exactly the same questions but in a polite and pleasant way?

Now compare the tone of the previous email with this email:

> Dear Lucy,
>
> I'm afraid[1] there are a few problems re the arrangements for the conference dinner:
>
> 1. FYI, the invitations have only just arrived this morning so I'm afraid I will be a day late sending them out. (This shouldn't make too much difference[2].)
>
> 2. Julia Winters called late yesterday. She was under the impression that 150 people were attending. Sujata's list says it's 170. Do you know[3] which of these figures is right?
>
> 3. Re the speeches, Alice and David are fine with 10 minutes each but Michael would prefer[4] 15 minutes. Is this possible? Also, I have heard that Saskia Winters would like to speak too. This may not be possible but I thought I'd let you know[5].
>
> Best,
> Ollie

Here the writer explains the same problems and asks the same questions without making the reader feel that the problems are all her fault! Notice how:

1 Before he tells her about a problem, he writes 'I'm afraid ...'
2 He tells her about a problem but lets her know that it is not serious.
3 He adds 'Do you know' to the question, which softens it.
4 He uses the polite phrase 'would prefer' rather than the direct verb 'wants'.
5 In the previous email he blames the reader, (you didn't ask Saskia to speak and she's offended). Here, he simply lets the reader know that there is a problem. She can then decide what to do.

Generally, people intend their emails to be **polite and pleasant** – or at least neutral. However, because emails are often brief and quickly written, they can sometimes sound slightly demanding, angry or even rude.

Remember that the reader of your email **cannot see you smile** and **cannot hear that your voice is friendly**. Try to be aware of this potential problem and to develop ways of showing that you are polite and friendly through the words that you write. This is *especially* true if the person you are emailing has never met you.

If you are emailing someone that you have spoken or written to before, consider starting your message by saying '**I hope you are well**'. Again, this lets the reader know that you are friendly and pleasant.

It is fine to keep your emails brief, but **not too brief**. You want to communicate quickly and efficiently but you still need to show respect to the reader and to show that you have considered their feelings. This can be difficult, especially when you are in a hurry, but it is important. If, for example, you are giving a piece of bad news, start your sentence with 'I'm afraid ...' or 'I'm sorry ...' rather than just stating the problem.

Be aware that verbs used in **the passive can sound a little formal**. For example 'The sales report that you were sent in February' (passive) sounds slightly formal whereas 'the sales report that I sent you in February' (active) does not. This is fine if you want to write a slightly formal email. If you are emailing a colleague that you know well, and want to write a friendlier email, however, you may want to avoid this structure.

Do not write using all UPPER-CASE LETTERS. People sometimes use upper-case letters to show the difference between their own writing and someone else's. This may make the reader think that you are angry and shouting. Upper-case letters are also more difficult to read than lower-case letters.

Always read an email that you have written before you send it, especially if you are writing to disagree with someone. **Imagine that you are the reader** and try to **read the email as they will read it**. Does it sound angry, aggressive or demanding and, if so, is that *really* what you intended? If you are in any doubt, do not send the email immediately. Save it and read it later in the day when you are feeling calm and can judge whether you need to change it.

> **Tip for success**
> Before you send an email, read it to check that the tone of it is what you intended.

Punctuation and abbreviations

Generally, the rules for spelling, grammar and punctuation that apply to letter-writing also apply to formal or work emails:

- Bad spelling, grammar and punctuation may give the reader a bad opinion of you and of your company, if you work for one.
- In addition, they may make your message unclear or confusing. In particular, emails that lack full stops or commas are difficult to read.

It is generally agreed that **contractions** (I'm, he's, can't, etc.) **are acceptable** in most formal or work emails. In formal *letters*, the full form of the words should be used but, as we have said before, formal emails are less formal than formal letters.

Other abbreviations, such as 'U' for 'you', 'plz' for 'please', and 'tx' for 'thanks', though often used in personal email, are generally not acceptable in formal or work emails.

Likewise, emoticons or smileys ☺ are not generally used in formal or work emails:

- They are considered too informal or 'familiar'.
- There is a risk that the reader will not understand what you mean by these symbols.

Tip for success
Always read an email before you send it to check for errors.

Ending a formal email

Between the main part of the email and the 'sign-off', (the part that says goodbye), there is often a line linking the two.

What you write at this point will, of course, depend on the purpose of your email, but here are a few typical sentences that are often used here:

- *I hope to hear from you soon.*
- *I look forward to hearing from you.*
- *I look forward to your response.*
- *Many thanks for your time.*
- *Thanks again for this.*
- *Many thanks in advance.*
- *Thank you for taking the time to answer my questions.*
- *I hope this helps.*
- *Please do get in touch if you have any more queries.*
- *Please do not hesitate if you have any questions.*
- *Do let me know what you think.*

Just as it is a good idea to start an email with a greeting, it is also **polite to finish an email with a sign-off**. Not everyone does this: some people end an email by typing their name alone. But an email that ends without a sign-off can sound a little rude, especially if the content of the email has included a disagreement or problem.

A number of sign-offs are commonly used in formal or work emails. Again, there are no fixed rules for the type of sign-off that you use. The phrases below are some of the most common.

- *Many thanks*
- *Thank you*
- *Thanks again*
- *Best*
- *Regards*
- *Best regards*
- *Kind regards*
- *With kind regards*
- *Best wishes*
- *With best wishes*

Below is an example of a slightly formal email. The sender of the email, (an artist), is replying to a person who has made an enquiry about their work. They have never met each other. Notice the tone which is polite and friendly but still slightly formal.

Subject: paintings
From: "Lewis, Lara" <lara.lewis@pnc.co.uk>
To: "Michael Peters"

Hello Michael

Thank you for your enquiry.

I am a studio artist at Holler Arts Centre and am based at Portland, just west of Bristol. You are welcome to visit me there anytime and have a look at the paintings I have available (no obligation of course!).

I also attend events around the country as you can see in my 2010 Events page on my website.

Prices start at £150 for the small paintings (approx. 20 x 15 cm). The larger paintings are about £400 (50 x 40 cm) depending on the piece.

I also undertake commissions if you have something specific in mind.

Please give me a ring on 01209 459825 if you would like to come to my studio and we can arrange a suitable time.

Kind regards
Lara

This email is sent from one colleague to another. This time, as the sender and reader know each other, the tone is slightly less formal, though it is still formal enough to be suitable for work.

Subject: minutes, (meeting 20/03/15)
From: "Rose, Andrew" <andrew.rose@wentworths.co.uk>
To: "Helena Ghiotto"

Hi Helena,

I'm attaching the minutes from yesterday's meeting.

Thanks very much for coming to the meeting. I think we all found it very useful to have your sales perspective on the various issues. Sophia and I agreed that it would be good to have you or Chris present at such meetings in the future. Perhaps we could discuss this over a coffee sometime?

Would you mind emailing me a copy of Jeanne's report? Thanks in advance.

Have a good trip – and please say hi to Carlo from me.

Best,
Andrew

Informal or social emails

The rules for writing informal or social emails are very relaxed. Generally, when people email their friends, **they use the same sort of words and phrases that they use when they speak**. They often use abbreviations – there is a list of common ones on page 120.

Starting the email

People usually **start informal emails with a greeting** in order to sound friendly. Usually, people write '**Hi**' or '**Hi Julia**' or '**Hello Julia**'. '**Dear Julia**' is also common, but slightly more formal. Sometimes there is no greeting, and the name of the reader alone is used.

Ending the email

There are no fixed rules about how to end an informal email. In a very quickly written email, there may be no 'sign-off' (the part before the name that says goodbye). However, **most people do use a sign-off** as it is friendly. The following are all commonly used:

- *Love*
- *Lots of love*
- *Take care*
- *See you soon*
- *Cheers!*

Additionally, we often write another friendly phrase between the main part of the email and the sign-off. These are some examples:

- *Talk to you later.*
- *Hope you're all well.*
- *See you soon.*
- *Better go now.*
- *Tell you more when we speak.*
- *Have a good weekend.*
- *Hope to see you soon.*

Texts and online communication

Many people use forms of communication that are briefer than emails. Texting is probably the most common, but sending messages through other forms of social media such as **Facebook™**, **Snapchat™** and **WhatsApp™** is also very popular, especially among young people.

These kinds of communication are even more relaxed than emails. Abbreviations are common, and **capital letters are rarely used**.

Texts

Remember that texts will be read on a phone screen, so **keep them short**. It's not necessary to start with a greeting or end with a formal sign off. You only need to put your name at the end of the message if you think you will not be in the person's contact list. If you are, they will already know that the text is from you.

Predictive texting can save you time. This is where the machine tries to guess the word you want after you have typed a couple of letters. Be careful with this, though. Sometimes the guess will be wrong, and if you are typing quickly, it's easy to miss mistakes.

> **Key point to remember**
> Read through predictive texting before pressing 'send'.

Social media

Social media websites come in and out of fashion, but sites such as Facebook™ are extremely popular and are often used for things such as arranging social events.

Be certain that you understand how to use the **privacy settings**. These enable you to control who sees what you put on the site.

Twitter™

Twitter™ is a social media site which allows users to post short messages of up to 140 characters. These are called **Tweets™**.

Along with some other social media sites, it uses a **hashtag** system, where the symbol # is put before certain words in order to index them, so users can search for particular topics.

Twitter™ is often used to comment quickly on things that are currently happening. It is therefore very easy for people to post comments without considering them carefully. However, the normal laws of libel apply, which means that people can take legal action if something is written about them that is not true. The use of a pseudonym (a name that is not your real name) does not necessarily protect the writer from being traced.

Online forums and message boards

The internet allows a huge range of interaction, and many people use online forums for discussion or post messages on websites, for example, comments on online newspaper articles.

The rules for this kind of communication are generally fairly relaxed, but depend on the subject you are writing about – comments on a football match may be humorous, include slang, or be somewhat impolite, whereas comments on a piece of serious journalism may be more formal.

You should be aware that if you intend to persuade someone of a particular opinion, bad spelling and grammar could weaken your message, because readers may not respect your view as much as they would if you wrote more 'correctly'.

Many sites have **moderators**, who will remove messages they feel to be offensive, or which do not conform to the site's policy.

Remember that if you respond to someone else's post, your post may not end up next to theirs, and this can be confusing to readers. Many people copy the section of post they want to respond to into their own post, so that it is clear what they are talking about.

Abbreviations and emoticons

It is very common in informal electronic communication to use abbreviations. These are some of the most common ones. Some people write them using capital letters in emails, but lower case letters are increasingly used, especially for texting or quick messaging.

@	at	**gr8**	great	**r**	are
2	to/two	**hth**	hope this helps	**rofl**	rolling on the floor laughing
2day	today	**ic**	I see	**spk**	speak
2moro	tomorrow	**idc**	I don't care	**sry/soz**	sorry
4	for	**idk**	I don't know	**ttyl**	talk to you later
afaik	as far as I know	**idm**	I don't mind	**thx/tx**	thanks
asap	as soon as possible	**im(h)o**	in my (humble) opinion	**ty**	thank you
atm	at the moment	**irl**	in real life	**u**	you
brb	be right back	**l8**	late	**ur**	your/you're
btw	by the way	**l8r**	later	**w8**	wait
cu	See you.	**lol**	laughing out loud	**wbu**	What about you?
cya	See ya!	**m8**	mate	**wrk**	work
fwiw	for what it's worth	**nm/nvm**	never mind	**wuu2**	What are you up to?
fyi	for your information	**omw**	on my way	**y**	why
g2g	got to go	**pls**	please		
		pov	point of view		

Emoticons (also called **smileys**) are often used in informal messages. These symbols represent emotions, for example ☺ for happy, ☹ for sad, and 😉 to show you are joking.

Many systems allow you to pick from a wide range of emoticons, some of which have movement when sent (e.g. a waving hand). Some can be represented with punctuation, for example ;-) to show you are joking (the semi-colon represents a wink). Many systems will change the punctuation into a real emoticon when the message is sent.

Formal or work letters

Nowadays so much communication is done through email and the telephone that the skill of formal letter writing can get forgotten. However, letters are still used in some situations.

Here is a general layout for a formal letter. Note that the layout of formal letters varies but that this format is generally accepted.

7 Molden Rd
Bristol
[1]BR2 4UP

[2]18 November 2015

[3]Ms Harriet Jones
Planning Officer
Bristol City Council
Bristol
BR1 3GY

[4]Dear Ms Jones,

[5]**Planning Application Ref. No. 09/291/XUL**

Thank you for your letter informing us of this application. As the owners and occupiers of no.7 Molden Road, we are concerned that the creation of five new houses will create an unacceptable degree of noise and disturbance in the area.

We are also anxious about the amount of traffic that this development will generate. As parents who cycle on Molden Road with our children, we feel that the extra volume of traffic will make the road unsafe.

For these reasons, we believe that this is a highly unsuitable proposal for development in this area, and hope that the Council will reject the application.

[6]Yours sincerely,

Anthony Johnson Sylvie Marks

[7]Mr Anthony Johnson & Ms Sylvie Marks

1 Write your address in the top right corner of the letter. Do not write your name here.
2 Write the date on the right, under your address. Write the month in full as a word.
3 Write the address of the person that you are writing to on the left, under your address and date.
4 If you know the name of the person you are writing to, use the title and the family name to address them. If you do not know the name of the person you are writing to, write 'Dear Sir or Madam'.
5 The heading goes here in bold, giving the subject matter of the letter. This will not be appropriate for all formal letters but is useful in cases where the letter clearly relates to a particular subject.
6 Write 'Yours sincerely' to end the letter if you know the surname of the person you are writing to. Write 'Yours faithfully' if you do not. Remember to start 'Yours' with a capital letter.
7 Write your signature by hand and then type your name under it. Put your given name first and family name second.

> **Key point to remember**
> If you know that the person you are sending the letter to is a woman but you do not know how she prefers to be addressed, use the title, 'Ms'. 'Ms' is used for both married and single women.

Most formal letters have a similar structure, having an introduction, a main part and a conclusion.

In your first paragraph, introduce the reason that you are writing. This should be brief – one line or two is usually enough.

> *On June 20th, 2015, I bought a self-assembly children's scooter (model: XR36) from you for £25 which I paid for with cash.*

In the main part of the letter **give details which explain the reason that you are writing**. Keep this as brief as you can. Say everything that you need to say but no more. Present the facts in a logical order that can easily be understood.

> *The next day I unpacked and assembled the scooter and my son rode it to the park. After half an hour of using the scooter, I noticed that the middle of the rear wheel was cracked. I immediately stopped my son from riding on the scooter as I was worried that it was unsafe.*

In the conclusion to your letter, **tell the reader what you would like them to do** as a result of your letter:

> *I am not at all happy with the quality of this make of scooter and am therefore requesting a full refund.*

The language that you use in a formal letter must be appropriate. It should be polite, whatever subject you are writing about. It does not need to be very formal but it **must not be *informal***. Do not use:

- slang or informal language
- contractions, such as 'I'm' and 'can't'

Make sure that you **spell the name of the person that you are writing to correctly**. People can feel offended when their names are spelled wrongly.

It is helpful to **write a clear heading** before the main part of your letter. This tells the reader exactly what the letter is about. There is a greater chance that the reader will pay attention to your letter if they know from the start what they are dealing with.

Take care over the appearance of your letter. Present the text in short blocks and leave plenty of white space between them. Prepare a letter that looks easy to read.

> **Key point to remember**
> Make sure that you use the reader's correct title. For example, do not write 'Mr ...' if the reader is a doctor and likes to be addressed with that title.

When you are planning your letter, try to **think of the contents of that letter from the point of view of the reader**. Most working people read a great deal of text every day, whether it is email, text messages or printed matter. Most people are also very busy in their jobs and have only a limited amount of time to read a message in whatever form it is sent.

You – the letter writer – must therefore try to help the reader by making the message of the letter as clear as possible. You can do this by:

- giving the main point (or points) first. Your reader will immediately want to know why you are writing to them and may feel impatient with your letter if they have to read through a lot of text in order to find this out.
- not including too much information. Only write what the reader needs to know. Do not include a lot of details or the reader may struggle to understand the main point of the letter.
- not including irrelevant information. This might confuse the reader or make them impatient.
- keeping your sentences short and simple. Short sentences with a simple structure are easier to understand.

> **Tip for success**
> Write a clear letter that can be easily understood.

Look at this letter written by the parent of a child to the child's teacher:

62 Acer Glen
Perth
WA6023

13 December 2015

Carine Glades School
Carine Avenue
Perth
WA6023

Dear Ms Lennon,

I am writing to clarify the situation regarding Millie's nut allergy as I know this has recently caused some confusion and concern. Millie has a slight allergy to almonds and hazelnuts. The allergy is mild and not life-threatening but it does cause swelling of the mouth which Millie finds distressing. Our doctor has recommended that Millie avoids eating all foods containing these nuts. If any of the children brings birthday cake or biscuits into school, please could Millie not be given any in case the food sets off an allergic reaction. In the event of Millie accidentally eating food that contains almonds or hazelnuts, please administer the medicine which the school office now has in their medicine box. This will immediately alleviate the symptoms. The medicine is clearly marked with Millie's name. I hope this clarifies the situation. If you have any questions at all, please call me on 57837 7293045. Many thanks for your help.

Yours sincerely,
Anna Green

Now see how much clearer and easier to read the letter is when:

- a heading is used, giving the reason for the letter
- the text is broken up into short paragraphs
- there is plenty of white space around those paragraphs

62 Acer Glen
Perth
WA6023

13 December 2015

Carine Glades School
Carine Avenue
Perth
WA6023

Dear Ms Lennon,

Millie Green's nut allergy

I am writing to clarify the situation regarding Millie's nut allergy as I know this has recently caused some confusion and concern.

Millie has a slight allergy to almonds and hazelnuts. The allergy is mild and not life-threatening but it does cause swelling of the mouth which Millie finds distressing. Our doctor has recommended that Millie avoids eating all foods containing these nuts.

If any of the children brings birthday cake or biscuits into school, please could Millie not be given any in case the food sets off an allergic reaction. In the event of Millie accidentally eating food that contains almonds or hazelnuts, please administer the medicine which the school office now has in their medicine box. This will immediately alleviate the symptoms. The medicine is clearly marked with Millie's name.

I hope this clarifies the situation. If you have any questions at all, please call me on 57837 7293045.

Many thanks for your help.

Yours sincerely,
Anna Green

Letters are sometimes written to make complaints, for example about the quality of goods or services. The following letter is written by a woman who is unhappy with the service that she recently received in a restaurant:

101 Richmond Street
Chatham, ON
N7L 1E1

17 June 2015

Maria's
160 King Street West
Toronto, ON
M5H 1J8

Dear Sir or Madam,

[1] I am writing to complain about the poor service I received in your restaurant, where my friend and I had lunch last Saturday (June 13th).

[2] Having requested over the phone a table by the window, we were disappointed to find ourselves seated instead at the back of the restaurant. Our food took over an hour to come and when it arrived, my friend's main course was cold. We complained about this and our waitress returned the food to the kitchen for reheating. Unfortunately, she forgot to bring the food back to us and, when reminded, was visibly impatient. Neither dessert that we chose from the menu was available and, although we asked for our coffees to arrive with dessert, they came ten minutes after it.

[3] As a result of all this, we did not enjoy our evening. Your restaurant had been recommended to us by a friend but I am afraid we were extremely disappointed by what we found.

[4] I am enclosing a copy of the bill and would like to receive a refund of at least half of it.

I look forward to hearing from you shortly.

Yours faithfully,

Carla Sylva

Carla Sylva

1. In the opening paragraph, explain briefly what you are complaining about.
2. In the main paragraph explain the problem, giving particular examples of what you are dissatisfied with. Include relevant details, such as dates and places. Give enough information here but not so much that the important parts are lost.
3. Tell the reader what the result of all these problems was.
4. Tell the reader what you would like them to do about the problem.

Be polite. Keep the tone of your letter polite and as pleasant as possible. You may feel that the reader is to blame for your situation but do not be rude to them. If the reader is offended by what you write, they will probably not want to help you with your problem. In any case, the person reading your letter will probably not have caused your problem.

Stay calm. You may be angry but try not to let this show. Never use an aggressive or threatening tone. Avoid adjectives such as 'terrible' and 'appalling' that cause or show strong emotion and use calmer, more neutral words. If you are openly angry with the reader, it is likely that they will feel angry with you.

People often apply for a job by sending to a company their CV together with a job application letter. With a well-written job application letter you can:

- point out the most important parts of your CV
- show a potential employer that you can write effectively
- show a potential employer that you are a pleasant person

16 Bezuidenhout Street
Troyeville
Johannesburg 2094

18 March 2015

Ms Helena Lewis
Human Resources Manager
Bigbook Publishing
Johannesburg 2094

Dear Ms Lewis,

[1]**Editorial assistant**

[2]I am writing to apply for the above post as advertised in the Evening Standard on March 14. I am enclosing my CV, as requested.

[3]I am currently working in a publishing company that specializes in children's books. [4]I have been working on various aspects of publishing, including editing, liaising with freelance editors and checking manuscripts.

I have worked in this company for two years and have gained considerable experience and knowledge. [5]I now feel that it is time to take my career to the next step. I am looking for a position that will provide new challenges and engage me more fully in the publishing process. [6]I am organized and energetic and I enjoy meeting and working with a range of people.

[7]I would welcome the opportunity to discuss my CV with you.

I look forward to hearing from you.

Yours sincerely,

Thomas van Leeuwen

Thomas van Leeuwen

1 Give the title of the job that you are applying for here.
2 Give details of the job that you are applying for and say how you found out about it.
3 Describe the job that you are doing now, including details of tasks and responsibilities.
4 Tell the reader what skills and knowledge you have gained in your current job.
5 Tell the reader why you want to leave your current job for the new job.
6 Describe the qualities that make you suitable for the new job.
7 Say that you would be pleased to provide the reader with more information.

Do not write too much in your letter of application. The main part of the letter should have two or three short paragraphs only. Ideally, the whole letter should only be one page.

Write a job application letter for each new job that you apply for. Do not assume that a general letter of application will be enough. Write specifically about the job that you are applying for and keep in mind the skills and qualities that are right for that job.

Tip for success
Always address a letter of application to a particular person. If you know the title of their job but not their name, call the company and ask for their name.

The following is a letter of enquiry, written by a person who is looking for work. It is not a response to a job advertisement. Instead it is the sort of letter that a person who wants work sends to several potential employers, hoping that one of them will require their services:

3 Victoria Street
Wellington 6011

6 August 2015

Hotel Grand
26 Quay Street
Auckland 1021
BR2 4UT

Dear Sir or Madam

I am writing to enquire about the possibility of work in your hotel this summer. I am especially interested in reception duties but would seriously consider any other type of work that you could offer me.

I am a twenty-year-old student and for the last three years have spent every summer working in hotels in Wellington. I have worked as a receptionist, a waitress and a cleaner. This summer I intend staying with relations in Auckland from December 5th till January 31st and am hoping to find employment for this period.

I enclose a CV giving details of my work experience and very much look forward to hearing from you.

With thanks.

Yours faithfully

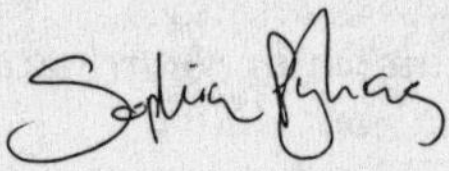

Sophia Pylas

Informal letters

Again, so much communication is done through email and the telephone these days that informal letters between friends are becoming quite rare. Still, some people like to write letters – or at least notes – to their friends. There are also some occasions when, even between good friends, a letter seems more appropriate than an email.

> 1 *18th December, 2015*
>
> 2 *Dear Sara,*
>
> 3 *It was great to speak to you last week – thanks for phoning. I'm so sorry I haven't been in touch this year. It's been quite hectic with one thing and another!*
>
> 4 *We're both really excited that you're coming to see us in the new year – it's been far too long. I just thought I'd better remind you to bring your walking boots. There are some fantastic walks we can do round here (if we have the energy!) Also, make sure you bring warm sweaters and coats. The scenery here is gorgeous but it is very cold, especially in January, (and I seem to remember from our college days together that you feel the cold!)*
>
> *Did I mention I bumped into Steve Washington in Manchester earlier this year? He looked so different I almost didn't recognise him. Anyway, I'll tell you more when I see you ...*
>
> 5 *Really looking forward to seeing you both. I'll call you nearer the time with directions.*
>
> 6 *Much love,*
> *Emma* 7 *xxx*
>
> 8 *PS Can't wait to see you with short hair!*

1 You do not need to write your address here, although some people do. If you want to give the reader a new or different address, you can write it here. If you sometimes write from one place and sometimes another, you may show which of these addresses you are writing from by putting, for example:

London
8th December, 2015

2 You can use the traditional greeting for an informal letter, which is 'Dear Paolo/Greta, etc' or you may like to write simply, 'Hi Paolo/Greta, etc'.

3 You can start an informal letter by referring to a previous communication with the reader. You can also start by asking after the health of the reader or by saying sorry for not having written to or telephoned the reader recently:

- *How are you?*
- *How are you doing?*
- *I hope you're both well.*
- *I'm sorry it's been so long since my last letter.*

4 The tone of an informal letter is very often conversational. Just as in conversation, you can use informal words and phrases freely. You can use contractions (e.g. 'I'm', 'won't', etc) too and you do not have to write in full sentences.

5 You can end a letter by saying how pleased you are that you are going to see the reader soon. You may also encourage the reader to write or to call you:

- *It'll be great to see you.*
- *It would be great to meet up one of these days.*
- *Can't wait to see you.*

- *Hope to hear from you soon.*
- *Stay in touch.*
- *Write soon.*

6 If you are writing to a close friend, before you sign your name, you will want to show affection by using a word or phrase such as:

- *Love,*
- *Lots of love,*
- *Much love,*
- *All my love,*
- *Love from,*

If you are writing to a friend that you do not know so well, you may prefer:

- *Best wishes,*
- *All the best,*
- *Kind regards,*
- *Regards,*

7 If you are very close to the reader, you can add a kiss or kisses after your name (X or XXX) or a hug or hugs (O or OOO).

8 If, when you have finished writing you letter, you think of something else that you want to add, you can put it after the letters, 'PS'.

Letters are still sometimes written to mark special occasions. For example, here is a letter congratulating the reader on getting a new job:

Leeds
3rd July

Hi Channa,

How are you doing? I'm just dropping you a line because I wanted to say congratulations on landing your exciting new job!

Dan and I are both very pleased for you. You told us last time we met up that you were looking around but didn't seem very optimistic about the opportunities. I know there are a lot of people out there chasing not many jobs. You must have been pretty impressive in interview!

Anyway, I just wanted to congratulate you. I hope the job is everything you want it to be and that you get to work with a great bunch of people.

Well done, Channa!

Lots of love, Sharmaline and Dan
xxx

Notice that the letter, though informal, follows the basic structure for formal letters. It has:

- an introduction where the writer says why she is writing the letter, i.e. to congratulate the reader on getting her job.
- a main part, where the writer puts background information, writing that she knew the reader was looking for a new job and that she knew finding work was difficult
- a conclusion where the writer congratulates the reader again and adds two specific wishes of her own

Another occasion which often makes people feel that they should write letters is the death of a person loved by the reader. People often feel that the seriousness of the occasion deserves a proper letter and not a quickly written email. A letter, rather than a phone call, also gives the writer time to think about what they want to say and how they are going to say it. This can be a very hard letter to write.

> *Stratford*
> *13th June 2015*
>
> *Dear Polly*
>
> *I'm writing because I've just heard the very sad news about your dad. I just wanted to tell you how sorry I am and to let you know that I am thinking of you.*
>
> *I have very fond memories of Colin. He was a very kind, warm man and always so welcoming when I came to visit. You enjoyed such a good relationship with him and remained so close throughout your adult life. I know you will be devastated by his death. I am very sorry. I know Ben will be a great comfort to you at this difficult time.*
>
> *Thinking of you, Polly, and sending you all my love.*
>
> *Julia*

Again, this letter follows the introduction – main part – conclusion format.

- an introduction where the writer says that she has been told that the person has died.
- a main part, where the writer relates good memories of the dead person and says they know how important the person was to the reader. This part also often includes something that the writer hopes will comfort the reader.
- a conclusion where the writer usually says that they are thinking of the reader.

Blogs

A blog is a website where someone regularly writes their thoughts and opinions in the form of a *post*. Blogs usually contain text, images and links to other websites.

Blogs are written for various different reasons. Many people write blogs in order to comment on political issues or stories in the news. Some bloggers write about particular activities and all the issues that relate to them, while other people write blogs in order to sell a product or service. Some blogs, meanwhile, just describe what the blogger does in their daily life.

The style and tone of a blog will depend very much on its content. A cycling blog written by a keen cyclist might have an informative and factual tone. The blog writer, (*blogger*), wants to provide useful information for other cyclists and to share their experiences with them. They may not be so interested in entertaining their readers.

A political blog, on the other hand, might be very funny, using humour in order to criticize politicians.

The blog that someone writes about their daily life will probably have an informal tone and be written in the style of a conversation, 'chatting' to its readers as if they were friends.

Whatever the content or subject matter of the blog that you are writing, there are a few general rules.

The first – and possibly the most important – is to **consider your reader**. **Who** do you intend to read this? What are their interests and opinions, and **what do they want from your blog**? Do they want:

- information on a particular subject?
- entertainment?
- to hear your opinions?
- all of the above?

It is only by providing what your reader wants that you will keep them coming back for more.

It might help to **think of your blog as a *resource*** for the reader. For example, if you are writing a blog about a particular sport, you might like to **share tips** with the reader about techniques that you have discovered that have improved your performance. Or you might **provide links** to websites that sell equipment that you have found useful. Give your reader the advantages of your experience and knowledge.

> **Key point to remember**
> If you give links to other blogs or websites, make sure you have visited them first and are certain of their content.

Talk to your reader. Most blogs are written in a slightly informal, conversational English. This is what readers expect. It gives them the feeling that they have formed a relationship with the writer and are connecting with them. Try to imagine that you are *chatting* to your reader. **Use the sort of words and phrases that you would naturally use in conversation** with a friend. This may include words and phrases that you would not use in other forms of writing.

Be yourself. People want to read blogs with original writing and original ideas. If they come back to your blog, it is because they like reading about what *you* have to say and they want to see how *you* say it. Be confident in your style and never try to write like someone else.

Do not be afraid to start your sentences with 'I'. Generally, people do not expect blogs to read like newspapers. In other words, they do not visit a blog to read a report of facts. Most people read blogs because they give them a chance to learn about other people. They want to know *what the writer has done* and *how the writer feels* about things.

Tell your reader in the first person about your experiences and opinions.

> **Tip for success**
> Once you have developed a style of writing that you are happy with, keep using that style.

Keep your blog short. Most people spend only a few minutes of their day or week reading blogs. They simply do not have time to read a lot, no matter how interesting or amusing the writing is. Do not fill the screen with text. Leave some white space and create a clean, simple screen that the reader knows they can deal with quickly.

Write a post that readers can scan. Remember that many people who visit a blog do not read the whole text word for word. Instead they *scan* the screen, looking for particular words and phrases. They may want to get the general idea of what you have written or they may want only to find particular information. Present your blog in such a way that people scanning the text can get the most from it. You can do this by:

- writing in **short paragraphs**. It is much easier to scan a text that is broken up into many short *chunks* rather than one long block of text.

- providing **lists of information**, introduced by bullet points. Lists are quick and easy to understand.

- providing a number of **relevant titles** to break up your text. Titles naturally attract the eye and can help guide the reader to a particular part of the post.

Communicate your message quickly. Whatever message or information you are trying to communicate in your post, make sure you do it within the first few lines. Do not assume that the reader has the time or the interest to read through a long introduction. Start your point immediately you start writing.

Make use of pictures. Select attractive and relevant images to break up blocks of text. Even if your images are only for decoration, they will still make the screen look more professional and more appealing.

Finally, when you have finished writing your post, **edit your writing**. The tone of your blog might be relaxed and informal but you still need the writing itself to be correct. Some readers will stop visiting a blog because the English is poor even though they are interested in the topic. Take time to:

- remove phrases or words that are not needed
- change the order of paragraphs if this improves the post
- correct errors
- correct punctuation

> **Key point to remember**
> Get your reader's attention by saying what is most important within the first few lines.

Essays

Writing essays is difficult and a lot of people struggle with some aspect of it. However, there are a number of things that you can do to make the task easier.

Give yourself enough time. In order to write the best essay possible you will probably need to read about the essay topic and research it. All of this takes time. Writing an essay hours before you have to hand it in is very stressful and rarely results in an excellent essay. Help yourself by starting your essay well before the deadline.

Learn from others. Read essays that other people have written on a range of subjects. Consider:

- How does the writer introduce the topic?
- What phrases do they use to present their points?
- How have they linked those points?
- Do they present their points in a logical order?
- Does the conclusion successfully bring together all the ideas and points presented in the essay?

Has the writer succeeded in any of the above and, if so, what can you learn from this?

Never plagiarize. If you use someone else's words, always give the name of the person who wrote or said those words and the title of the work in which the words appeared. Never pretend that someone else's words are your own.

Read and then re-read the essay title. Before you start even to plan your essay make absolutely sure that you understand the title and what it is asking you to do. Remember that this is one of the main points on which your essay will be judged. This point may sound obvious but failure to answer the question is one of the commonest reasons for essays being marked down.

As you write more essays, you will notice that certain verbs are used again and again in essay titles. Here are some of the most common of these, together with their meanings. Make sure that you know exactly what each verb means in the context of an essay title:

- **analyse**: to examine something in detail for the purposes of explaining it
- **assess**: to judge how valuable, important or successful something is
- **compare**: to look for similarities between
- **contrast**: to look for differences between
- **evaluate**: to judge how valuable, important or successful something is
- **illustrate**: to explain something by using examples
- **outline**: to describe the most important points
- **relate**: to show how two or more issues are connected
- **summarize**: to describe the most important points

Key point to remember
No matter how well written your essay is, if you fail to answer the question, you will lose marks.

Take time to **plan your essay**. Proper planning will help you to organize and develop your thoughts so that you are clear about what you want to write. It will also ensure that you do not leave anything out. Planning does not need to take a lot of time, and there are a number of helpful and imaginative ways that you can do it. There is a section on planning your work near the beginning of this book.

Keep to the point. Do not introduce unrelated subjects or aspects of a subject that are not relevant. Even if your points are interesting, you will not gain marks for them! Ask yourself before you make each new point, how does this point answer the essay title?

Make every word count. Write clearly and concisely, avoiding over-long sentences and unnecessary adjectives. You will want to show that you have a varied vocabulary but do not be tempted to use a lot of words where a few well-chosen words will do!

Remember paragraphs. As a general rule, every time you make a separate point, start a new paragraph. Do not make your paragraphs too long. If a paragraph is very long, consider dividing it into separate points.

Remember that the type of English that is right for essays is a **slightly formal English**. It is more formal than the English that we usually use for speaking and writing emails. The English generally used in essays does not:

- include informal or slang words (unless you are quoting someone).
- include contractions, such as 'isn't' and 'won't'.
- generally include phrases that use the words 'I', 'me', or 'my'.

Finally, when you have finished your essay, make sure you **read it carefully at least twice**. Be prepared at this point to make changes to it. Consider:

- the order of the points that you make. Is this logical and does the essay 'flow'?
- your choice of language. Is it clear and does it say exactly what you intended it to say?

Look out too for:

- spelling errors
- repetition of particular words. If you find you have used a word many times, consider replacing it with a synonym (a word with a similar meaning).

Tip for success
Use your computer's spellchecker to check your finished work but make sure that you read your essay for spelling errors too. Remember that a spellchecker will not find a typo such as 'from' where the intended word is 'form'.

Essay phrases and words

There are **different stages to an essay** and each stage of the essay requires you to do different things. Under the relevant heading below, you will see a range of words and phrases that can be used at a particular stage or for a particular purpose. Use these words and phrases to express your ideas in a way that is more precise and more varied.

Introductions

The following notes will help you with many of the issues you need to cover in your introduction:

Introducing the topic and purpose of an essay
Here you **say briefly what you will discuss**, making sure that it fits exactly with the title of your essay:

- *This essay will examine/look at ...*
- *This essay focuses on/discusses ...*
- *This essay considers/explores*
- *The aim of this essay is to assess/examine ...*
- *This essay seeks to evaluate/examine ...*

Defining key terms used in the essay
If there is any doubt about the meaning of a word or phrase that is important in your essay, **explain** in your introduction **what *you* mean** by that word or phrase:

- *Throughout this essay the term 'x' will refer to ...*
- *The term 'x' refers here to ...*
- *For the purposes of this essay, the term 'x' is used to mean ...*

Explaining how the essay is organised
You may like to give a very **brief summary of the structure** of your essay. This shows the teacher/examiner that you have arranged your thoughts and arguments in an organized way. It will also make it easier for them to understand exactly what you are saying:

- *This essay has been divided into three parts. The first part looks at ...*
- *There are three parts to this essay. The first part deals with ...*
- *This essay has been structured in the following way.*
- *This essay begins by... It then looks at ...*
- *The first part of this essay examines/looks at ...*

Saying why the topic is particularly interesting or important
You may like to **put the topic in context**, especially if the topic is of particular relevance now:

- *It is often said that...*
- *We live in a world in which...*
- *The issue of x is one that affects everyone ...*
- *Recent years have seen an increasing interest in ...*
- *The past decade has seen the rapid growth of ...*
- *One of the most important developments in recent years is ...*

Raising an area of your topic where there is disagreement or controversy
You might like to **offer arguments against** a statement in the essay title, especially if you know of recent findings that seem to contradict it.

- *This is not always true, however.*
- *This is not always the case, however.*
- *However, recent evidence suggests that this may not be the case.*
- *More recently, research has emerged that seems to contradict ...*
- *Concerns have been recently been raised about ...*
- *There is increasing concern about ...*
- *Not everyone agrees with this statement, however ...*
- *Not everyone is in favour of x, however ...*

Mentioning an area of your topic where there is a lack of knowledge
Again, this offers you the opportunity to introduce an argument against a statement in the essay title or to at least to **show that there is doubt about the subject**.

- *Less is known, however, about the effects of ...*
- *So far there has been little discussion of ...*
- *However, very little attention has been paid to ...*
- *We hear a lot about x but we hear less about y.*

The main part of the essay

This is the part of the essay where you **discuss and develop the ideas** that you outlined in your introduction. In this part of the essay, you will need to do several things, for example, give facts and make statements, justify or disagree with statements, give reasons and suggest causes. The following notes will help you with many of the issues you need to cover in the main part of your essay:

Stating what is generally considered to be true
You will probably want to **introduce a statement that everyone – or most people – agree is true**. (You might then develop the point or go on to argue against that point.)

- *It is often said that ...*
- *It is certainly true that ...*
- *It is certainly the case that ...*
- *It is undoubtedly the case that ...*
- *No one would argue that ...*
- *Few people would argue that ...*
- *Few would argue that ...*

Stating that something is partly true

You may **only partly agree** with a statement:

- *There is an element of truth in this statement.*
- *There is some degree of truth in this.*
- *This is to some extent true.*
- *This is to some degree true.*

Key point to remember

When giving personal opinions in academic essays, it is generally better to avoid phrases that use the words 'I', 'me', or 'my':

✗ *I think that keeping animals in captivity is wrong for the following reasons.*
✗ *It's my opinion that keeping animals in captivity is wrong for the following reasons.*
✓ *Keeping animals in captivity is wrong for the following reasons.*

Providing facts

You might like to **refer to some new information** or statistics that relate to your topic:

- *Recent research clearly indicates/shows ...*
- *Recent research suggests ...*
- *A new study confirms that ...*
- *A recent report revealed ...*
- *It has recently emerged that ...*

Useful words and phrases

The verbs 'seem' and 'appear' can be used to make these claims less definite, for example:

Government-funded research into this area appears to/seems to confirm this theory.

Suggesting reasons for something

You might want to **suggest an explanation** – or more than one explanation – for a situation or problem that you have described:

- *Perhaps this is because ...*
- *It might be that this is caused ...*
- *This may be because of/caused by ...*
- *This may be a result/consequence of ...*
- *It is likely/possible that ...*
- *We might assume from this that ...*
- *One possible explanation is that ...*
- *We might deduce from this that ...*

Describing the result of something

If you have stated the cause of something, you might want to **say what the result is**. These words can be used to start sentences that link the cause of something with the outcome.

- *Consequently ...*
- *As a result/consequence ...*
- *The result is ...*
- *The consequence is ...*
- *It follows that ...*
- *Therefore ...*

Adding to a point that you made before

You might like to **add to a previous point**, either by saying something that you think is **equally important**:

- *Besides, ...*
- *In addition, ...*
- *Similarly, ...*
- *In the same way, ...*

or by giving a point that is **even more important**:

- *What is more, ...*
- *Furthermore, ...*
- *Moreover, ...*
- *More importantly, ...*

Introducing examples
You will almost certainly want to **provide examples of what you are claiming**. Examples provide proof for your claim and can be introduced with the following words:

- *For example ...*
- *For instance ...*
- *A good example of this is ...*
- *An illustration/instance of this is ...*

Useful words and phrases
Alternatives to the phrase '*good example*' are '*notable example*' and '*prime example*'.

Note that you can vary the structure of your sentences by sometimes using the phrases 'for example' and 'for instance' in the middle of a sentence, with commas before and after:

- *Paper recycling, **for example**, is now common practice in most countries.*

- *Cycling to work, **for instance**, can significantly reduce your carbon footprint.*

You may want to highlight the importance of one particular example, in the following way:

- *Environmental issues, **particularly/in particular** global warming, dominate the news.*

- *Environmental issues,* ***notably/chiefly*** *climate change and recycling, are at last being addressed.*

Giving different opinions
Whatever your view on a subject, you will probably need to **show that you are aware of different views**, with phrases such as:

- *It could/might be argued that ...*
- *It is sometimes said that ...*
- *There are those who claim that ...*
- *Some claim that ...*
- *Another way of looking at/viewing this is ...*

Discussing differences
You may want to **highlight the differences** between two things:

- *There is a marked/sharp contrast between ...*
- *x is in sharp/stark contrast to y*
- *There is a clear distinction between x and y*
- *There are significant differences between x and y*
- *This contrasts sharply with ...*
- *x differs/varies widely*
- *By/In contrast, ...*
- *By/In comparison, ...*
- *Conversely, ...*

Key point to remember
Remember that the phrases '*in contrast*', '*by comparison*' and '*conversely*' can appear in the middle of a sentence, (with commas before and after), as well as at the start of a sentence, e.g.:

Carlos was clever, handsome and charismatic. His brother, in contrast, was a plain, shy man.
Carlos was clever, handsome and charismatic. In contrast, his brother was a plain, shy man.

Reporting what someone else has said

You will sometimes want to **quote what someone else has said or written**. There are many reasons for doing this. You might want to provide support for your own opinion or you may want to introduce an opinion that you can then disagree with.

- *Smith asserts/claims/proposes/suggests that ...*
- *Smith maintains/states that ...*
- *Jones comments/observes/remarks/reports/writes that ...*
- *Jones concludes that ...*
- *According to Jones, ...*
- *As Jones states/points out, ...*
- *In Jones's view/opinion, ...*
- *Jones's view/opinion is that ...*

> **Key point to remember**
> Note that the present tense is usually used in such phrases.

Introducing quotations

Often, you will need to **name not only the author of a quotation, but also the piece of writing** that the quotation comes from. This can be done in a number of ways so it is a good idea to ask your teacher if there is a recommended style:

- *Blake (1998, p. 62) asserts that "Walker hated his mother".*
- *Blake[1] claims that "Walker hated his mother".*
- *As Blake (1998, p. 62) points out, Walker had a difficult relationship with his mother.*
- *Blake (1998, p. 62) maintains that Walker had a difficult relationship with his mother.*

Saying the same thing in a different way

You will sometimes want to **make clear exactly what it is that you are saying** by repeating your point in a way that is briefer and simpler.

- *In other words, ...*
- *To put it simply, ...*
- *To put it more simply, ...*
- *That is to say, ...*
- *To look at this another way, ...*

Conclusions

The conclusion brings together all the ideas and information you have discussed. It shows the reader that the essay is complete and that the aims of the essay have been achieved. In a conclusion, you **summarize the main points** and say what the consequences of your evidence are:

- *In summary, ...*
- *To summarize, ...*
- *To sum up briefly, ...*
- *In conclusion, ...*
- *To conclude,...*
- *It can be concluded that ...*
- *We can therefore conclude that ...*

Dissertations

A dissertation is a **long piece of writing on a particular subject**, especially one that a student does as part of their university degree. It is usually divided into a series of numbered chapters.

A dissertation is like an essay in that it is **formal in style**. The type of language that is suitable for essays is also suitable for dissertations. It does not:

- include informal or slang words.
- include contractions, such as 'isn't' and 'won't'.
- generally include phrases that use the words 'I', 'me', or 'my'.

For help with formal writing, especially phrases and words to use in dissertations, see the part in this book on writing essays.

A dissertation is **very much longer than a normal essay**. It can be anything up to 10,000 words long.

It has a **more complicated structure** than an essay. This is partly because it is so much longer and partly because it examines its subject in greater depth. It is important to note that the exact structure of a dissertation will vary depending on:

- the area of study of the dissertation. Different subjects require different structures.
- the university that you belong to, or the department within that university. Different universities have different rules on how to structure a dissertation.

Key point to remember
Before you even start to plan your dissertation, make sure you have a copy of your university (or university department's) rules on how to structure a dissertation.

As we have said, the structure of a dissertation will vary, depending on the university and the subject. It is your responsibility to make sure you know exactly what your university or subject requires. The general features of the structure that are given here are therefore only a rough guide:

Title Page

Among other details, this page will include:

- the title of the dissertation
- the name of the writer
- the qualification for which the dissertation has been written
- the relevant university or other place of study
- the date that the dissertation was submitted

Table of contents

This is an index of everything that is contained in the dissertation except the title page and the table of contents.

Abstract

This will say in general terms what the dissertation is about. An appropriate length is generally agreed to be about 300-500 words.

Main part of the dissertation

This will be divided into sections or chapters. The sections or chapters will each have an introduction, a main part and a conclusion. However, it is very important that there is a link between these subsections. When you are writing this part of the dissertation, try to remember that the reader must at all times understand how one part relates to another.

Conclusion

This is where you help the reader to understand the significance of your conclusions, rather than just restating your conclusions. It can be a challenging part of the dissertation to write. Some people find it helpful to write this part of the dissertation a little time after the main body of the text. This allows them to think more clearly about everything that they have written and to make judgements about it.

Bibliography
This should be a complete list of the books and articles, etc. that you have used in your dissertation.

> **Tip for success**
> Do not delay preparing your bibliography until the end of your dissertation. Prepare it as you are writing your dissertation.

Dissertations are complicated pieces of work and are not easy to write. You can help yourself with this challenging task by **planning the structure of your dissertation very thoroughly**. You will want to show the plan to your supervisor before you start to write it. Your discussions with your supervisor will very often result in changes to your plan so **allow yourself plenty of time for the planning stage** of the process.

For general help with planning a piece of writing, see the section on planning near the beginning of this book.

When you are ready to start writing, **do not assume that you must start at the first chapter and finish with the last**. Many people find that there is an area of the dissertation that they are more confident about. Consider starting with that area of the subject.

Most universities have a set of rules about how to present a dissertation. These rules concern, for example, the type and size of font used, the type of paper written on and the layout of the page. **Make sure that you have a copy of the presentation guidelines for your university and that you follow them**.

The **rules for good writing apply to dissertations** as they do to any other form of written work. For general help with formal writing, see the chapters in this book on writing essays and writing reports. It is worth repeating some of these rules here as they are especially true of long, complicated pieces of writing, such as dissertations.

Write clearly. You know what you mean by your writing but if you do not express yourself clearly your reader may not. Make sure your reader does not have to struggle to understand your English.

Write concisely, avoiding over-long sentences and unnecessary adjectives. These will make your English difficult to follow.

Avoid repetition. If you find you have used a word many times, consider replacing it with a synonym (a word with a similar meaning).

Remember paragraphs. Text should never appear as a long block. As general rule, every time you make a separate point, start a new paragraph.

Write paragraphs of the right length. They should not be too long or too short. Never write a paragraph of only one sentence.

> **Tip for success**
> Remember your reader at all times. Try to write English that is a pleasure to read.

You will almost certainly want to **write more than one draft of your dissertation**. Re-writing is an extremely valuable part of the process. It can be hard to see where the problems are while you are writing a piece of text. It is only when you come back to the text that you see where changes need to be made. You may find at this stage that you need to:

- explain a point more clearly
- remove a point that is not relevant
- change the order of the points that you are making

The above changes all relate to the content of your dissertation. As well as examining the content of your dissertation, you will also need to **check it thoroughly for errors**.

Remember that a supervisor who has read parts of your work will only have commented on its content or structure. They will not have brought to your attention spelling or grammatical errors. Use your computer's spellchecker to check your finished work but make sure that you **read your dissertation for spelling errors too**. Remember that a spellchecker will not find a typo such as 'from' where the intended word is 'form'.

Tip for success
Give your dissertation a separate read-through in order to check for grammatical errors and spelling errors.

Reports

A report is a **written document which presents information about a particular subject** to a particular reader or group of readers. The writer of the report has usually been asked by the reader to prepare the report.

Reports are written by people who work in many areas, for example business, government and education.

All **reports present a number of facts** which the writer examines in detail. The writer then makes judgments based on those facts. Many reports also make recommendations about things that should be done because of the facts that they have described.

Before you start writing a report, make sure that you **know exactly what it is that you want to achieve**. It may help you to form a clearer idea if you write a short paragraph describing the purpose of it.

Make sure too that you **know exactly who you are writing the report for**. You may be writing for readers with the same understanding of the subject and the same interests, or you may be writing for different types of reader. Your report will need to cover everything that your readers are expecting.

Like an essay, a report is a **formal piece of writing**. The type of English that is right for reports does not:

- include informal or slang words
- include contractions, such as 'isn't' and 'won't'.
- include words that show or cause strong emotions, such as 'horrible' and 'atrocious'

- generally include phrases that include the words 'I', 'me' or 'my'. (However, note that if the report includes recommendations, this part of the report may use such phrases.)

Although the English in your report should be formal, it should also be **clear and *readable***. 'Formal' is not the same as 'difficult'. You want your reader to **understand quickly** what you have written without having to make a lot of effort. Although it may not be possible to write a report that your reader actively *enjoys* reading, you do not want the reader to *struggle* to get through it!

Do not use long, difficult words in order to impress the reader. The use of a lot of long words can have the effect of making your writing less readable. Most readers prefer plainer, more direct English. For example, if you find yourself writing the verb 'utilize', consider whether the simpler verb 'use' could be used instead. Likewise, if you write 'dwelling', ask yourself whether 'home' would in fact be better.

Do not write long sentences. Of course you will want to write some longer and some shorter sentences in order to provide some variety in your English. However, you should try to avoid very long, complicated sentences as they are difficult to understand. Look at the following sentence:

> In terms of numbers, this is essentially an increase, albeit a small increase, and we look forward to seeing this trend continue over the forthcoming weeks and months.

Now see how a shorter sentence can say the same thing much more clearly:

> This is an increase, albeit a small one, and we look forward to seeing this trend continue.

Notice in the first sentence, the phrases and words:

- in terms of
- essentially
- over the forthcoming weeks and months

These words and phrases have *little or no meaning* in this sentence. In the second sentence, the writer has removed them without changing the meaning. If you have written a long sentence, examine the various parts of that sentence and consider whether any of the words are not needed.

As we have said, the main purpose of a report is to present facts about a subject. The purpose is *not* to describe the writer's opinions or feelings on the subject. For this reason, **do not use the words 'I', 'me' or 'my' in your writing**. You may need to suggest ideas and give possible explanations for certain facts, but you should not do so with phrases such as 'it seems to me' and 'in my opinion'. Compare the sentences below:

> ✗ *The same quarter saw sales in these markets rise by 13 percent, a development which I am convinced is due to better marketing of these products.*

> ✓ *The same quarter saw sales in these markets rise by 13 percent, almost certainly as a result of better marketing of these products.*

Similarly, the language that you use in your report:

- should not *show* your feelings
- should not *cause* strong feelings in your readers

For this reason, avoid words such as 'appalling', 'terrible' and 'fantastic'. Instead use adjectives which express the same idea but in a calmer, more formal way. Compare these sentences:

✗ *Sales for the last quarter of the year were terrible.*
✓ *Sales for the last quarter of the year were very disappointing.*

✗ *This was a fantastic achievement.*
✓ *This was a remarkable achievement.*

Remember that some people will not want to read the whole report, word for word. Instead they will want to *scan* it, getting the general idea of what you have written or looking for particular information. Present your report in a way that **allows people to read it quickly**. Consider:

- writing in **short paragraphs**. It is much easier to scan a text that is made of many short *chunks* rather than one long block of text.

- giving information in the form of **bullet points**. Bullet points are quick to understand and are an acceptable way of presenting information in reports.

- breaking up your text with **headings**. Headings will guide the reader to the parts of the report that they are interested in.

The main purpose of a report is to present information. Unlike an essay, a report does not always present information in the form of written paragraphs. You can show information very effectively in the form of **bullet points, tables, diagrams and charts**. Label any tables and diagrams, etc. clearly. Information shown in this way should relate to the writing in your report, for example:

Figure 1 shows that overall sales increased by 3% in the third quarter.
Overall sales increased by 3% in the third quarter (see Figure 1).

The structure of a report

The **structure of your report** will partly depend on what is contained in the report. However, most reports have a fairly similar structure:

1 Title page
2 Contents list
3 Executive summary or 'abstract'
4 Introduction
5 Main part of the report
6 Conclusions
7 Recommendations
8 Appendices
9 Bibliography

1 Title Page
Include the following formation in your title page:

- The title of the report
- The purpose of the report
- Your name and the name of the person that you have written the report for
- The date that you sent or gave the report to the reader

2 Contents list
If you have written a long report, you will need to provide a contents list. This gives the main sections and chapters of the report and the pages on which the reader will find those sections and chapters.

3 Executive summary or 'abstract'
In the executive summary or abstract, you need to give a **summary of the report**, describing briefly the most important information that is in it. The summary should not be long – about ten percent of the total report. As a rough guide, write one sentence for every main section of your report.

4 Introduction
Here, you should give the following information:

- Any background information relating to the subject that the reader should be aware of
- The purpose of the report
- Exactly which areas of your subject you deal with in the report

5 Main part of the report
This is the longest part of the report, where you say:

- What you discovered when you examined this subject
- What you decided was true after considering all the facts (the conclusions)

You will probably need to divide this part of the report into sections. Each paragraph or group of paragraphs on the same subject is a section. It is likely that each section will also need dividing into subsections. These sections and subsections will need to be numbered. The system used by most report writers is as follows:

- Each section in the main part of the report is numbered 1,2,3, etc.
- Sections within those main sections (subsections) are then numbered 1.1, 1.2, 1.3, 1.4, etc.
- If there are any subsections of those subsections, they appear as 1.1.1, 1.1.2, etc.

6 Conclusions
This is the stage at which you bring together all the conclusions that you reached in the main part of your report. Present these conclusions in the order in which they appeared. **Do not include any new information** here.

7 Recommendations

Some reports do not include recommendations. They present and examine facts but do not make suggestions about what should be done because of those facts. Some reports do include recommendations and set them out here, in a separate part of the report. Note that some reports include recommendations in the conclusion or even in the executive summary.

8 Appendices

This is the place to put information which is referred to in the report but is too detailed or complicated to include in the main part of the report. The sort of information you would put here includes:

- questionnaires
- long, detailed tables of figures
- any instructions for research referred to in the report

9 Bibliography

If you refer to a book in your report, give the following information here about that book:

- The author's or authors' name(s)
- The book's full title
- The name of the publisher and place where it was published
- The year it was first published or, the number of the edition and the date it was published

Finally, when you have finished writing your report, **read it carefully from beginning to end**. Be prepared at this point to make changes to it. Consider:

- the order in which you have given the facts. Is it logical?

- the conclusions that you have reached. Are they reasonable, considering the evidence that you have given?

- your choice of language. Is it clear and does it say exactly what you intended it to say?

If possible, leave your corrected report and come back to it a day later. Are you still satisfied with every part of it? Is there any part that you now feel you need to change? **Many people write several drafts of a report** before they are happy with it.

While you are re-reading your report, look out too for:

- typos and spelling errors
- repetition of particular words. If you find you have used a word many times, consider replacing it with a synonym (a word with a similar meaning).
- Unnecessary words. Look out for words which mean nothing. For example, a word such as 'basically' may have no meaning in a sentence.

Report phrases and words

There are **different stages to a report** and each stage of the report requires you to do different things. Under the relevant headings below, you will see a range of words and phrases that can be used at a particular stage or for a particular purpose. Use these words and phrases to express your ideas in a way that is more precise and more varied.

Introductions

Introducing the topic and purpose of the report

Here you **explain the purpose of your report** and say exactly which areas of the subject your report deals with:

- *This report will examine/look at ...*
- *This report aims to/sets out to examine*
- *This report focuses on*
- *This report considers/explores*
- *The aim/purpose of this report is to assess/examine ...*
- *This report seeks to evaluate/examine ...*
- *This report begins by ... It then looks at ...*
- *The first part of this report examines/looks at ...*

Defining key terms used in the report

If there is any doubt about the meaning of a word or phrase that is important in your report, **explain** in your introduction **what *you* mean** by that word or phrase:

- *Throughout this report the term 'x' will refer to ...*
- *The term 'x' refers here to ...*
- *For the purposes of this report, the term 'x' is used to mean ...*

Raising an area of the subject where there is disagreement or controversy

You might like to **offer arguments against** something that people generally think is true.

- *This is not always true, however.*
- *This is not always the case, however.*
- *However, recent evidence suggests that this may not be the case.*
- *More recently, research has emerged that seems to contradict ...*
- *Concerns have been recently been raised about ...*
- *There is increasing concern about ...*
- *Not everyone agrees with this statement, however ...*
- *Not everyone is in favour of x, however ...*

Mentioning an area of the subject where there is a lack of knowledge

You might want to **raise an area of your report's subject that little is known about**:

- *Less is known, however, about the effects of ...*
- *So far there has been little discussion of ...*
- *However, very little attention has been paid to ...*
- *We hear a lot about x but we hear less about y.*

Referring to new information

You might like to **refer to some new information or statistics** that relate to the subject of the report:

- *Recent research clearly indicates/shows ...*
- *Recent research suggests ...*
- *Recent findings suggest ...*
- *A new study confirms that ...*
- *A recent report revealed ...*
- *It has recently emerged that ...*

> **Useful words and phrases**
> The verbs 'seem' and 'appear' can be used to make these claims less definite, for example:
>
> *These recent findings appear to/seem to confirm this theory.*

Main part of the report

This is where you describe exactly what you discovered when you examined the report's subject:

Suggesting reasons for something
You might want to **suggest an explanation** – or more than one explanation – for a situation or problem that you have described:

- *Perhaps this is because ...*
- *It might be that this is caused ...*
- *This may be because of/caused by ...*
- *This may be a result/consequence of ...*
- *It is likely/possible that ...*
- *We might assume from this that ...*
- *One possible explanation is that ...*
- *We might deduce from this that ...*

Describing the result of something
If you have stated the cause of something, you might want to **say what the result is**. These words can be used to start sentences that link the cause of something with the outcome:

- *Consequently ...*
- *As a result/consequence ...*
- *The result is ...*
- *The consequence is ...*
- *It follows that ...*
- *Therefore ...*

Adding to a point that you made before

You might like to **add to a previous point**, either by saying something that you think is **equally important**:

- *Besides, ...*
- *In addition, ...*
- *Similarly, ...*
- *In the same way, ...*

or by giving a point that is **even more important**:

- *What is more, ...*
- *Furthermore, ...*
- *Moreover, ...*
- *More importantly, ...*

Discussing differences

You may want to **highlight the differences** between two things

- *There is a marked/sharp contrast between ...*
- *There is a clear distinction between x and y*
- *There are significant differences between x and y*
- *This contrasts sharply with ...*
- *x differs/varies widely*
- *By/In contrast, ...*
- *By/In comparison, ...*
- *Conversely, ...*

Key point to remember
Remember that the phrases 'in contrast', 'by comparison' and 'conversely' can appear in the middle of a sentence, (with commas before and after), as well as at the start of a sentence, e.g.:

Group A suffered few colds and infections. Group B, in contrast, reported constant ill-health.
Group A suffered few colds and infections. In contrast, Group B reported constant ill-health.

Reporting what someone else has said
You will sometimes want to **quote what someone else has said or written**:

- *Smith asserts/claims/proposes/suggests that ...*
- *Smith maintains/states that...*
- *Jones comments/observes//remarks/reports/writes that ...*
- *Jones concludes that ...*
- *According to Jones, ...*
- *As Jones states/points out, ...*
- *In Jones's view/opinion, ...*
- *Jones's view/opinion is that ...*

Key point to remember
Note that the present tense is usually used in such phrases.

Introducing quotations
Often, you will need to **name not only the author of a quotation, but also the piece of writing** that the quotation comes from. This can be done in a number of ways:

- *Blake (1998, p. 62) asserts that "Rogers was at fault here".*
- *Blake[1] claims that "Rogers was at fault here".*
- *As Blake (1998, p. 62) points out, Rogers was at fault here.*
- *Blake (1998, p. 62) maintains that Rogers was at fault here.*

Conclusions

Summarizing

You will want to **summarize the main points of your report**:

- *In summary, ...*
- *To summarize, ...*
- *In conclusion, ...*
- *To conclude, ...*
- *It can be concluded that ...*
- *We can therefore conclude that ...*
- *The following points summarize our key findings:*
- *The key findings are outlined below:*
- *It is clear that ...*
- *No conclusions were reached regarding ...*

Recommending

You may want to **advise the reader that something should be done**:

- *We strongly recommend that ...*
- *It is my recommendation that ...*
- *It is essential that ...*
- *It would be advisable to ...*
- *I urge x to ...*

Writing presentations

Why write a presentation?

The process of writing your presentation will help you to **decide** the **key points** of your talk so that you know exactly what you want to say. Deciding what to include – and what *not* to include – is very important and the key to a successful presentation.

As you write your talk, you will think of the most **logical order** in which to present your main points.

You will also make sensible decisions about what **slides** or other **visual aids** you need for your talk.

By writing the whole of your presentation in advance, you can make sure that your talk is the **right length**. It is no use preparing a brilliant talk that you cannot possibly give in the time allowed. On the other hand, you do not want to finish your talk twenty minutes early!

Giving presentations can be stressful and most people feel anxious about talking to large groups of people. If you know that you have **prepared your presentation properly**, it will give you confidence on the day.

Key point to remember
Don't leave it to the last minute to prepare your presentation. Have your presentation finished at least 24 hours in advance.

Deciding the content

Whatever your presentation is about, before you start writing it, ask yourself the following question: **What am I trying to achieve with this talk?**

The best way to be clear about this is to ask two questions:

1 **Who** is this presentation for?
2 **What** is my key message?

Who?
Always write a presentation that is suitable for your audience. Try to find out in advance as much as possible about the audience and what they will **expect from you**. If possible, speak to someone else who has given a presentation to the same audience, or at least speak to the person who has organized the talk. It will help you to plan your talk if you know the following about your audience:

- How much knowledge of your subject they have
- Their level of education
- How old they are
- How long they are able or willing to listen to a speaker

What?
The **key message** is the main thing that you want your audience to learn from your talk – or very often, the main two or three things. Before you even start to write your talk, decide what your key message is.

While you are thinking of the **purpose of the talk**, consider these questions. Is the purpose of this presentation:

- to **give your audience information?**
- to **persuade your audience to do something, for example to buy something?**
- to **entertain?**
- to **allow the audience to get to know you?**

Most presentations are intended to give the audience information. If this is your main purpose, make sure you **give the right amount of information**: too much and your audience will be unable to take it in; too little and your audience may feel that they have wasted their time.

It may not be appropriate to entertain your audience – this will, of course, depend on the subject that you are speaking about. However, when you are planning your talk, keep in mind that most people find it hard to concentrate when a speaker makes no attempt to keep their interest.

Key point to remember
Remember that if you entertain your audience, you will be more likely to persuade them or inform them!

When planning a presentation, it is useful to break it down into three parts: **the beginning, the middle and the end**.

In the beginning part of your talk, try to get your audience's attention. You might ask them to do a short activity or perhaps ask them a question. Choose something that will wake them up and involve them. **Make your audience listen to you!**

In the middle part of the talk, **tell them the facts** that they need to know. Keep it simple and limit yourself to what is really important. Do not tell your audience more than they can understand and remember.

Be aware that the last part of your talk is possibly the most important part. The audience are more likely to remember what you tell them at the end of your presentation than in the middle. Whatever your **key message** is, make sure that you **say it – or repeat it – at the end**.

Key points to remember
Involve your audience.
Repeat your key message in the last part of your presentation.

Writing notes for a presentation

Make good notes to help you give your presentation. Very few people can give a full presentation without looking at their notes now and then. Audiences do not expect speakers to be able to do this. Write only the **main points** of your talk on **numbered postcards or 'prompt cards'**. Write one or two key points on each card and make the writing bigger and clearer than your usual handwriting. There are several good things about prompt cards:

- They remind or 'prompt' you to say your next point but you do not read from them. Audiences like you to **look at them** and **speak to them**. A speaker who looks down and reads their notes will not keep their audience's attention.

- They allow you to **see your next point very clearly**. (When you have finished saying one point, put the card to the bottom of the pile and you will see your next point.)

- You can **write the time** that you should get to each point **on each card**.

Writing slides for a presentation

Always **prepare your own slides** so that you know exactly what is on them and will be able to use them with confidence and authority.

Keep the **text** on your slides **simple and brief**. Make sure your audience can make sense of them very quickly. Limit the amount of text on a slide to **six or seven words on each line** and to **six or seven lines of text** per slide.

It is important also to write the text of your slides **big enough to be seen**. Remember that if you are speaking to a lot of people in a large room, the people sitting at the back will need to be able to read your slides too.

It is a good idea to write a short **title** on each slide. This should be a single word or a short phrase. The purpose is to let your audience see immediately the subject of the slide. Make sure that your **titles** are **large** – larger than the rest of the text.

Edit your slides carefully. Look over them several times, checking the spelling and the phrasing. It is embarrassing to be told by a member of the audience that there is an error on one of your slides!

Webinars

Webinars are presentations that are delivered online so that people in different locations can use their computers to take part. They can be a powerful tool to bring together audiences from all over the world.

A webinar can take several forms. It can be a single speaker presenting to an audience, an interview or panel discussion between several speakers listened to by an audience, or a fully interactive discussion/training session, etc. between a small group of people.

A common format for a webinar is to have a speaker whose live image is visible in a small window. The speaker's slides take up the majority of the screen.

The audience logs on with a link and password that has been given to them. Members of the audience can write comments as the webinar progresses, and these comments can be seen by all participants.

A skilled presenter may be able to skim the comments pane while talking, but this can be distracting, and, with a large number of participants, it would not be practical. It is therefore a good idea for a webinar presenter to have an **assistant** who can react to comments coming in.

A knowledgeable assistant can give answers to questions while the webinar is still taking place, and can pick out questions for a question and answer session at the end. They could also alert the presenter to relevant reactions or misunderstandings from the audience.

Tips for webinars are the same as for more conventional presentations, but if anything, it is more important to keep your audience interested – it is much easier to walk away from a computer screen mid-presentation than it is to get up and leave a lecture hall!

Tip for success
Use an assistant to keep track of audience comments.

Presentation phrases

There are **different stages to a presentation** and each stage of the presentation requires you to do different things. Under the relevant heading below, you will see a range of words and phrases that can be used at a particular stage or for a particular purpose. Use these words and phrases to express your ideas in a way that is more precise and more varied.

Introducing yourself (and thanking your audience)
If you are new to presentations, it is a good idea to **write your introduction out in full on a prompt card**. Of course, you know this information yourself, but you may be very nervous at the start of your talk. It is easy to forget what you are saying when you are nervous. A written reminder of your first few lines will give you confidence:

- *Thank you very much for coming here today.*
- *First of all, I'd like to thank you all for coming here today.*
- *I'd like to start by thanking x who invited me here to give this talk today.*
- *My name is Paola Sanchez and I'm the marketing manager for Now Systems.*
- *My name is Paola Sanchez and I'm here today to talk to you about ...*
- *Let me introduce myself. My name is Paola Sanchez and ...*

Introducing your talk
It is a good idea at the start of a presentation to tell your audience in a few words **what you are going to talk about**. If your audience have a clear understanding of what you are talking about from the start, it will help them to understand the whole of the talk:

- *Today/This afternoon I'm going to be talking about ...*
- *My subject today is ...*
- *The topic of my talk is ...*
- *I'm here today to tell you about ...*
- *My aim this afternoon is to ...*

You might then **tell your audience about the structure of your talk**. Again, this will help with their understanding:

- *First, we're going to take a look at ...*
- *After that, we'll be considering ...*
- *Finally, we'll be thinking about ...*
- *I'm going to divide this talk into four parts. The first part deals with ... The second part looks at ... etc.*

Useful words and phrases
Notice that a speaker will often say '**We're** going to consider/look at, etc.' This makes the audience feel *involved* in what the speaker is saying.

'Reminding' people
You will be stating facts in your presentation. Your **audience may already know** some of those facts. It is a good idea to show that you are aware of this:

- *As you know ...*
- *You may be aware that ...*
- *You may have heard of ...*
- *I'm sure many of you will already know ...*
- *It's often said ...*

Referring to slides and other visual aids
It is likely that you will use slides or other visual aids as a part of a presentation. Try to **make a clear link between the slide and what you are saying**. The following phrases will help with this.

- *If you could just take a look at this slide ...*
- *This slide shows you ...*
- *This slide represents ...*
- *As you can see from this graph ...*
- *Looking at these figures, we can see that ...*

Giving more details

Often, in a presentation you make one point and then want to **give further details about that particular point**:

- *I'd like to say a little more about this point ...*
- *I'd like to add at this point that ...*
- *Another relevant point here is ...*
- *While we're on the subject of x, it's worth also saying ...*
- *Let's consider/look at this in more detail ...*
- *I'd like us to think about this for a moment ...*

Changing the subject

At various points in your presentation, you will want to make a new point. **Introduce each new point clearly**:

- *I'd like to move on now to the issue of ...*
- *Moving on now to the subject of ...*
- *Turning to the issue of ...*
- *Let's turn now to the subject of ...*
- *The next issue I'd like to think about/focus on is ...*
- *Now we'll move on to the subject of ...*
- *Let's look now at the issue of ...*

Using questions to make a point

You can **introduce a point by asking a question**. This might be a general point or a point that will especially interest the audience:

- *So, how does this relate to us?*
- *So why is this of interest?*
- *So why have I brought this to your attention?*
- *So why is this an advantage/a benefit?*
- *How much will all of this cost?*
- *What does this mean for ...?*
- *And why is this important/significant?*
- *So where does this lead/take us?*

Key point to remember
Introduce each new point that you make clearly.

Paraphrasing (saying something in a different way)
You may want to make a point clear by **expressing something in a different way**. These phrases will help:

- *In other words ...*
- *So what I'm saying is ...*
- *To put it another way ...*
- *To put it more simply ...*
- *Another way of putting this is ...*

Returning to a point you made earlier
You might want to **show how a new point relates to an earlier point** in the presentation:

- *As I said before ...*
- *Going back to what I said earlier ...*
- *To return to a point I made earlier ...*
- *Earlier in the talk, I mentioned ...*
- *You'll recall I mentioned x earlier ...*
- *This relates to a point I made earlier about ...*
- *Let's look back at something I said earlier ...*

Tip for success
Linking a new point with something you said earlier will help your audience to understand your presentation.

Summarizing your presentation
Towards the end of your talk, you may like to **remind your audience of the main points** you have made:

- *We've covered a lot of ground today. Let me quickly summarize the main points ...*

- *Let's summarize briefly what we've looked at today ...*
- *I'd like to quickly go over the main points of today's presentation ...*
- *If I can just sum up the main points of the presentation ...*
- *To finish, I'd just like to remind you of some of the issues we've covered today ...*

Concluding

Now is the time to **tell your audience the thing – or the things – that you want them to remember**:

- *I'll conclude very briefly by saying that ...*
- *I'll finish by saying ...*
- *Let me end by ...*
- *I'd like to leave you with this thought ...*

Finishing a presentation

Most speakers like to **let their audience know that they have finished their presentation**:

- *I think that's everything I wanted to say today.*
- *I think I've covered everything I wanted to say today.*
- *I think that's about it.*

You will then want to **thank your audience** and, if there is time, **invite them to ask you questions** relating to the subject:

- *Thank you all very much for taking the time to listen to this presentation.*
- *Does anyone have any questions (or comments)?*
- *Would anyone like to ask any questions?*
- *Please feel free to ask questions.*
- *If anyone has any questions, I'd be very happy to answer them.*
- *We have ten minutes left now if anyone has any questions they would like to ask.*

> **Tip for success**
> Always let your audience know that you have finished your presentation and remember to thank them for listening.

CVs

A CV, (curriculum vitae), is a document that you send to someone when you are applying for a job. It gives details of your qualifications and of the work that you have done in the past and are doing now. It also gives your full name and contact details. 'CV' is the word used in British English. In American English, this document is called a résumé.

People usually send a *cover letter* or *letter of application* with their CV. You will find help with this type of letter in the part of this book on writing letters.

CVs vary in length. In the UK, it is generally agreed that **two or three pages of A4** is about the right length. In the US, the résumé tends to be shorter, many people recommending that it should be no longer than **one side of A4**.

Whether you are writing a one-page document or a two- to three-page document, there are a number of things that you must keep in mind. The first of these is that the reader of your CV will probably assess your CV along with *many* others. They will probably have limited time to do this. Therefore, your CV must be:

- quick and easy to read
- clear and concise
- pleasant to look at

Key point to remember
Keep your CV concise. The reader will not have time to read through five or six pages, no matter how impressive the details.

Remember that if your CV is poorly presented, the reader will be more likely to reject it even if your skills and experience make you the perfect candidate for the job. Your CV must therefore have:

- a **clear structure**. Be sure to organize the information under headings such as *profile* and *experience*.
- **plenty of white space**. A dense page with too much text is difficult and unpleasant to read.

Make sure too that you write your CV on **good quality, clean paper**. Remember that the reader does not know you. The only evidence that they have of your character and your suitability for the job is the CV they have in their hand. Make it look impressive.

Remember that the information you include must be **relevant** to the work. Do not be tempted to include facts that do not directly relate to the job that you are applying for. A reader with little time to assess several CVs might be distracted by this and may not actually see the important information.

Key point to remember
Presentation is extremely important in CV writing. Two CVs with the same information will be judged differently by the reader if one CV is very much smarter and better organized than the other.

Here is a general layout for a CV. The structure and layout of CVs varies but this format is generally accepted. Notice the clear headings and the white space around the paragraphs.

[1]Helena Shapur

[2]12 Green Lane, Brighton, Sussex, BT1 3EY

Mobile 0779 234567 [3]h.shapur@xyz.co.uk

[4]Personal profile

An enthusiastic, self-motivated professional in the field of online team management, I have a passion for the potential of the Internet and an in-depth understanding of a wide variety of web technologies. I am committed to developing the same values and enthusiasm within my team.

[5]Career Summary

2012 – present Development Team Leader, Getaways.com

I joined this online travel company as a web developer, and in 2013 moved up to the position of Development Team Leader. During this exciting time, traffic to the site multiplied by more than 100 times. Working with a close-knit team, I gained real understanding of the nature of large-scale website management.

2008 – 2012 Web developer, Toprank Recruitment, Brighton

Having gained a taste for web technologies, I joined this small start-up, developing an IT recruitment website. Programming the site's search engine, I learned ASP, Javascript and SQL. I also gained valuable experience of developing a website as part of a team.

2006 – 2008 Junior Programmer, Oakleaf Processing, Manchester

As part of a small team, I developed and coded accounts and customer databases for clients. At the same time, I taught myself HTML and designed a new website for the company.

[6]Education and Qualifications

2003-2006 Merseyside University, BSC Computer Science (2:1)

2001-2003 Prince of Wales Sixth From College, Brighton 3 A-levels

1988-2003 St James High School, Brighton 9 GCSEs

[7]Hobbies and Interests

I am an avid reader and film-goer. I like cooking, gardening and writing children's stories.

[8]Referees

(professional)	(personal)
Martin Walker	Elizabeth Joachim
Toprank Recruitment	12, Cotswold Ave
Mill Street	Whalleyrange
Brighton BN2 34Y	Manchester MU32 6TF

1 Give your name in full at the top of the CV where it can easily be seen.
2 Give your contact details just below your name.
3 Always provide your email address.
4 Write a personal profile at the top of your CV. In two or three sentences, summarize the skills and personal qualities that make *you* the person for this job. Try to link your skills and qualities directly to what you have recently achieved at work.
5 Always provide details of your most recent employment first and then work backwards.
6 Likewise, provide details of your most recent qualifications first and work backwards.
7 The reader will want to get some sense of what you are like as a person, so do include brief details of your interests, especially if those interests are relevant.
8 Most employers expect to see details for two referees (= people who will give information about your abilities or character).

Instructions

You will see instructions on signs in public places, in recipe books, in operating manuals, on packets of food and a variety of other places.

Instructions are generally **written using the imperative form** of the verb. The imperative is formed by using the infinitive form of the verb without 'to':

> *Keep off the grass*
> *Stop when lights show*
> *Now add the garlic and tomatoes.*
> *Shake before use*
> *Re-connect the plug to the power socket.*

Negative imperatives are generally formed by putting 'do not' or 'never' before the verb:

> *Do not open door while wash is in progress.*
> *Do not leave in bright sunlight.*
> *Never leave small children unattended.*

Notice that sentences that give instructions often leave out words that you would find in ordinary sentences. For example, they sometimes do not include articles ('the' or 'a'). Sometimes they leave out objects. For example, the sentence above reads, 'Do not leave in bright sunlight'. It does not say 'Do not leave *this item* in bright sunlight'.

Key point to remember
Instructions are generally not written as complete sentences and they do not show who must follow the instruction.

Think carefully about your readers before you start to write your instructions. Consider:

- How much or how little do they know about the task for which you are writing instructions?

- How old are they?

The answers to these two questions will help you to decide:

- The level of your instructions and **how many steps you include**. If the reader knows little or nothing about the task that you are describing, you may need to give instructions for every action that is required, even if some of the instructions seem very simple to you.

- How **simple or difficult the language of your instructions is**. Will they, for example, understand technical terms? If not, you will have to find a way of giving instructions that involves simple language that anyone could understand.

- Whether you need to **add warnings to your instructions** for younger readers. For example, in a recipe you may need to warn the reader that a food is hot at a particular point and they must not touch it. Or you may decide to tell the younger reader to ask an adult for help with a particular action.

When you are writing instructions, make sure that they are **easy to follow**. Make them as **clear** and as **simple** as possible. Remember that the reader will be using your instructions because they have not done a particular task before.

Use **short, simple sentences**. Long sentences are hard to follow and can confuse the reader. Compare the following instructions for making chocolate fridge cake:

✗

Recipe 1

Melt butter in pan and add cocoa, sugar and syrup, bringing to the boil then remove from heat and stir in broken biscuits, mixing well. Press mixture into tin then melt chocolate in microwave, (medium power for 15 seconds), spreading the chocolate when melted evenly over the surface using palette knife and refrigerate before slicing.

✓

Recipe 2

Melt butter in pan.
Add cocoa, sugar and syrup to pan and bring mixture to the boil.
Remove from heat and stir in broken biscuits. Mix well.
Press mixture into tin.
Melt chocolate in a microwave, (medium power for 15 seconds).
Spread melted chocolate evenly over the surface using a palette knife and refrigerate before slicing.

Recipe 1 is confusing and difficult to follow for the following reasons:

- It uses long sentences. It gives you ten instructions in just two sentences. This is too much information for the reader to take in.

- It gives some instructions in a form that is not the imperative. For example, it uses the ing-form of the verb 'bring' in 'bringing to the boil' and not the clearer 'bring to the boil'.

- It relies on words such as 'then' and 'and' to tell the reader the order in which they should do different things. This is hard for the reader to understand and remember.

Recipe 2 is clear and easy to follow:

- It breaks up the ten instructions into seven short sentences.
- The reader can easily see the order of those instructions as each new step starts a new line.
- It uses the imperative form, (melt the butter, remove from heat, press mixture, etc.), for every instruction.

Key point to remember
Avoid using the passive form, ('be verb-ed') when writing instructions. The active form is clearer:

✗ The red button is pressed to start the wash cycle.
✓ Press the red button to start the wash cycle.

It is helpful to **give instructions as a list** rather than a paragraph. A list clearly separates the different actions that the reader must do and makes the instructions easier to follow. Your list may be numbered, or may have bullet points:

Grill from frozen in 8 minutes
1. *Preheat grill to moderate heat.*
2. *Remove all packaging.*
3. *Place on the base of a grill pan and grill for 5-7 minutes.*

Planting your seeds
- *Fill your pot with compost.*
- *Spread the seed over the compost surface.*
- *Water the compost generously.*

Think about the order of the actions that you are describing. Always give instructions for actions in the order in which you would perform them. This is not always as obvious or as easy as it sounds! Some actions can be performed at different stages of a task. Try to work out the most logical point at which to perform such actions. It can be helpful to write each step of a task on a different Post-it® note. You can then move the notes around until you have decided the most sensible order.

Consider **giving a title to your list of instructions**. The title should explain what the reader will achieve by following your instructions. You may want to make this sound exciting and appealing, especially if you are writing for children:

How to make the best chocolate brownies ever!
How to make a mask that will scare your mum and dad!

You may be writing instructions for a number of different but related tasks, for example, the different functions of a piece of equipment. It is useful here to **give short titles** for the various tasks, explaining what your instructions will help the reader to do. Note that the '-ing' form of the verb is usually used for titles like these:

Setting the Programme 'P'
Deleting/Changing the Programme
Cleaning the appliance

If the reader needs any items in order to perform your instructions, it is useful to **give a list of these items** before the instructions:

You will need:
2 pieces card (20cm x 20 cm)
glue
2 lengths thin ribbon (width 3mm)
sequins

Use helpful pictures or diagrams. Pictures and diagrams are especially useful:

- If the task for which you are giving instructions needs the reader to use different pieces of equipment or complicated equipment.
- If you are writing for children.

Choose your **pictures carefully**. Pictures or diagrams that are well-chosen and clearly labelled will show the reader immediately what things look like. (It can be difficult to describe in words the appearance of a particular thing or part.) They will also show how big or small one thing is compared with another thing. This can help to make sense of instructions. Make sure that your pictures or diagrams are:

- **clear and large enough** for the reader to see all the important parts.
- **clearly labelled**. If you are using lines to point to different parts of a picture, make sure the reader can see exactly which parts of the picture the lines are pointing to.

Tip for success
Give the right number of labels. Label the parts that the reader needs to know about but do not label every part.

You may find it helpful to **test your instructions** to make sure that they work. Test your instructions on people who have not seen your instructions before or have not done the task that you are describing. This will show you:

- where your instructions are not clear.
- where you have missed out an important step or piece of information.

Choose the people to test your instructions carefully – they should be typical of the sort of person who will be using your instructions. To learn the most from this activity:

- Ask the person or people to read through your instructions carefully and then ask them if they have any questions or comments.
- Ask questions that will show whether they have understood your instructions.
- If possible, watch the group try to perform the task by following your instructions. Afterwards, ask them how easy they found the task. Were there any instructions that they found confusing?

You can then rewrite any part of your instructions that was not clear or give instructions for any part of the task that was missing.

Leaflets and flyers

A leaflet or flyer is a printed sheet of paper that gives information about something. Leaflets are given to a large number of people free of charge.

Leaflets do a variety of things. They may simply give information, for example on a particular health problem, or on the refuse collection in a particular area. They may try to persuade people to buy a particular product or service, or they may try to persuade people to have a particular belief.

Whatever the purpose of a leaflet, all leaflets have a few features in common. **Leaflets are small**. Most are just one sheet of paper, sometimes folded in two. (This is necessary as they will be picked up, quickly read, and often then put in a pocket or bag.) Consequently, leaflets generally contain **only the most important facts** on a particular subject and they **communicate those facts in just a few words**.

When you are writing and designing a leaflet, keep in mind that people generally **look at a leaflet very quickly**. Remember:

- Include the most important information
- Do not include information that is not important
- Keep the text – or texts – short
- Express your points clearly so that they are easy to understand
- Include a telephone number/website address or other contact information

Before you start to write your leaflet, **draw a rough sketch** of how you want it to look. Plan where you are going to put the title, the words, and any pictures you are using.

Try to make the leaflet look attractive and choose an image or images that will capture people's attention. **The right image or images** will also **help to communicate your message**.

Do not put too much in your leaflet. Remember that people need to be able to read a leaflet quickly. If they think that your leaflet will take them too long to read, they may not even pick it up! **Leave plenty of white space** around the text and images.

You can design your leaflet in a number of ways, even if it is a single-sheet leaflet. For example, you could put just a title and image on the front of the leaflet and the words themselves on the back. You may decide to put both images and text on both sides of the leaflet. **Make these important decisions before you even start to write the text**.

Tip for success
Before you do anything else, plan the overall design of your leaflet.

When you have prepared an overall design for your leaflet, it is time to choose the words. The best way to do this is to try to **see those words through the reader's eyes**. Imagine the questions the reader might ask when they pick up your leaflet.

Your first task, therefore, is to work out **who your typical reader is**. It is only when you have worked this out that you can start to work on the words.

For example, imagine you are preparing a leaflet for a company that delivers boxes of organic fruit and vegetables to people's houses. The typical reader is a person who has at some point considered having a box like this delivered. The reader now wants to find out how your particular company would provide such a service. You can assume that the reader is interested in this type of service because one or more of these is true:

- They like good quality food.
- They care about the environment.
- They want to support small, independent companies.

They will therefore probably want answers to the following questions:

- How good is the food?
- Is it truly organic?
- How 'green' is the company?
- Who runs this company?

On the basis of these questions, the facts that you would want to include in your leaflet are:

- The food is of the highest standard – fresh and delicious.
- The food is grown according to strict organic standards, without pesticides.
- The company respects the environment in everything it does, for example in using only crops grown locally and in using very little packaging.
- This is a small, local, family-run company.

Other facts that *any* reader will want to know are:

- How much does it cost? (Are there different prices for different size boxes?)
- How convenient is it? (Can I choose what fruit and vegetables I have in my box?)

What is important is that you **remember to keep the reader's needs in mind**. *Only* include information that is interesting and useful to them. *Do not* be tempted to give a lot of detailed information.

Tip for success
Before you include information in your leaflet, ask yourself these two questions:

Will the reader want to know this?
Will the reader understand this?

When you know what information you want to include in your leaflet, you must decide how you are going to present that information. A list of **bullet points is a very clear way of presenting key information**. Look at the text in the following leaflet:

> *Greener Gardening – Local Garden Service*
>
> *We do all types of gardening tasks, including garden design, hedge trimming, garden maintenance, lawn maintenance, flower beds, tree & shrub planting and grass cutting.*

Now see how a list of bullet points can make the same information much clearer:

> *Greener Gardening – Local Garden Service*
>
> *We do:*
> - *Garden design*
> - *Hedge trimming*
> - *Garden maintenance*
> - *Lawn maintenance*
> - *Flower beds*
> - *Tree & shrub planting*
> - *Grass cutting*

Your leaflet may include the type of information that you cannot present in a list. For example, you may need to explain a number of facts, requiring you to write a series of paragraphs. If you are including a lot of information, remember to **break up the text with titles** for the different paragraphs.

Look at the text in the following medical leaflet:

> Symptoms of the virus may include a sore throat, headache, fever, loss of appetite or extreme tiredness. Call your doctor immediately if you are pregnant or your condition suddenly gets much worse. Some people are more at risk of serious illness if they catch the virus. At risk are people with long-term lung disease, heart disease and kidney disease.

Now see how titles can make the same information much clearer:

> **Common Symptoms**
> Symptoms of the virus may include a sore throat, headache, fever, loss of appetite or extreme tiredness.
>
> **Call your doctor immediately if:**
> You are pregnant or your condition suddenly gets much worse.
>
> **High-risk groups**
> Some people are more at risk of serious illness if they catch the virus. At risk are people with long-term lung disease, heart disease and kidney disease.

Get your reader's attention from the start. Make the first line of your leaflet count. For example, rather than starting the text by describing your company, you could present the reader with the problem that your product or service will solve. Look how one home-delivery pizza company starts their leaflet:

> *Sandro's Pizzas*
> *We deliver hot, tasty pizzas within a two-mile radius of Littleport.*

Now see how effective it can be to take a different approach, talking directly to the reader:

> *Paolo's Pizzas*
> *Hungry but had enough of cooking? We deliver hot, tasty pizzas ...*

Include quotations. If you are trying to sell a product or service with your leaflet, you may like to include quotations from previous satisfied customers (though first check with the customer that they are happy for this to happen!):

> *"The most delicious, authentically Italian pizzas I've ever eaten in this country!" (K Peters, Littleport)*

Use simple language. Keep the language of your leaflet simple. Never include technical terms that your readers may not know. Make the sentences short so that the leaflet can be read and understood quickly.

Provide the right contact details. Will the readers of your leaflet want to call you or go to your website? Do they need to know where your office is or how to email you? Make sure you provide the contact details that your reader needs.

Make your contact details clearly visible. Write them where the reader will see them. The top or bottom of a leaflet is usually clearer than the middle of a piece of text. Consider writing them on *both* sides of the leaflet.

Edit your leaflet. Remember that your leaflet is going to be read by members of the public and you need to create the best possible impression. The spelling, grammar and punctuation in your leaflet must therefore be perfect. Read and re-read your finished leaflet. If possible, arrange for someone else to check it.

Test your leaflet on a friend or colleague. Show them your leaflet for ten seconds only. Now ask them two questions, (getting the answer for the first question before you ask the second):

1 What was the main purpose of the leaflet?
2 Tell me three things you have learned from the leaflet.

Could your friend/colleague tell you the main purpose of the leaflet? Were the three things they learned from the leaflet the three *key* things that you want your readers to notice? If their answers were not what you were hoping for, consider re-writing parts of your leaflet.

Tip for success
Take time to prepare your leaflet properly. A badly written leaflet may do more harm than good no matter how many people read it.

Grammar, punctuation and spelling

PART THREE

Main verbs

Verbs are words that allow us to talk about activities, processes, states of being, and states of mind. You may have heard verbs referred to as 'doing words':

*This basket **holds** quite a lot.*
*John **was reading** Katherine's essay.*
*Anirban **is preparing** a talk for next week's class.*
*Eleni **feels** much happier now.*
*I **forgot** that it was your birthday.*
*Paul **owned** several old motorbikes.*

A **verb phrase** can be a single word or a group of associated words:

*he **walks***
*he **is walking***
*he **had walked***
*he **can walk***
*he **has been walking***
*he **might have been walking***

Transitive verbs are verbs which have to have an object:

like: *She **likes** cheese.* (You can't say just 'She likes.')
describe: *He **described** the house.* (You can't say just 'He described.')

Intransitive verbs do not have an object:

sneeze: *I **sneezed** loudly.* (You can't sneeze *something*.)
complain: *He's always **complaining**.* (You can't complain *something*.)

Many verbs can be **transitive or intransitive**:

> *Sales levels have* ***increased***. (intransitive)
> *We have* ***increased*** *our spending on training*. (transitive)
> *The fog made it difficult to* ***see***. (intransitive)
> *The fog made it difficult to* ***see*** *the mountains*. (transitive)

The **infinitive** form of the verb is the basic form that you would look up in a dictionary. For instance, if you wanted to look up the verb in this sentence:

> *She had* ***encountered*** *many problems.*

You would look up the **infinitive**, 'encounter', not 'encountered'. In different situations, the infinitive is used with or without 'to'. Without '**to**', it is called the **bare infinitive**:

> *The child was too small* ***to reach*** *the switch.*
> *I'm sorry* ***to hear*** *your news.*
> *I don't know how* ***to do*** *it.*
> *You must* ***lock*** *the door.*

Auxiliary verbs

Auxiliary verbs are used with main verbs in order to allow us to talk about different periods of time and to form questions and negatives.

Be and ***have*** are the **primary auxiliaries**. A primary auxiliary is used to construct compound tenses.

Be is used to make present continuous and past continuous tenses and for the passive:

> *I **am working**.*
> *We **were** all **wondering** about that.*
> *Martin **was arrested** and held overnight.*

Have is used to make present perfect and past perfect tenses:

> *Sasha **has finished** fixing the car.*
> *Amanda **had** already **eaten** when we arrived.*

Do is the **supporting auxiliary**. It is used in forming negatives, questions, and emphatic statements:

> *I **do** not **like** sausages at all.*
> ***Do** you **like** prawns?*
> *You **do like** prawns, don't you?*

Tip for success
In speech and informal writing, the auxiliary verbs 'be' and 'have' often join with their main verb to make a contraction, e.g. I'm, she's, they've.

Modal verbs

Modal verbs are used before other verbs to express ideas such as ability, possibility and necessity.

The main modal verbs in English are:

can	**could**	**may**	**might**	**must**
ought	**shall**	**will**	**would**	

Modal verbs are different from other verbs because they do not change their form:

*I **can** ride a horse.*
*She **can** ride a horse.*

In speech and informal writing, the modal verb **will** is often shortened to **'ll** (e.g. I'll, they'll) and the modal verb **would** is often shortened to **'d** (e.g. I'd, they'd).

Negatives of modal verbs are formed like this:

modal verb	***negative***	***short form***
can	*cannot*	*can't*
could	*could not*	*couldn't*
may	*may not*	*(mayn't is formal and very rare)*
might	*might not*	*mightn't*
must	*must not*	*mustn't*
ought	*ought not to*	*oughtn't to*
shall	*shall not*	*shan't*
will	*will not*	*won't*
would	*would not*	*wouldn't*

Phrasal verbs

A phrasal verb is a type of verb that is created when a main verb is combined with either:

- an **adverb**:

take off	*give in*
blow up	*break in*

- a **preposition**:

get at (someone)	*pick on (weaker children)*

- or an **adverb + preposition**:

put up with (insults)	*get out of (doing something)*

Often the meaning has nothing to do with the literal meaning of the verb or the particle (the adverb or preposition).

Tip for success
Although nouns that are formed from phrasal verbs (e.g. take-off, break-in) often have hyphens, you should not use hyphens between the parts of phrasal verbs.

Nouns

A noun is a word that labels a thing or an idea. Nouns are sometimes called 'naming words'.

Proper nouns are the names of people, places or things, and start with capital letters:

John Lennon *China* *Mount Everest* *Thursday*

Common nouns are all the other nouns that refer to things. They can be divided into the following groups:

- **Abstract nouns**. These refer to things that you cannot see or touch:

  honesty *anger* *idea* *time*

- **Concrete nouns** are things you can see or touch:

  dog *teacher* *stone* *sugar*

A concrete noun may refer to a living thing (**animate** noun) or a physical object (**inanimate** noun).

Collective nouns refer to collections of people or animals:

*a **herd** of cows*
*a **swarm** of bees*

Compound nouns are nouns made from two or more words. Some are written as one word, some as two words, and some with a hyphen:

teapot *washing machine* *break-in*

Many compound nouns have more than one acceptable form (e.g. stomach ache/stomachache). Check in a dictionary if you are not sure.

Countable and uncountable nouns

Countable nouns refer to things that we can count: *one cat*, *two cats*, *seventeen cats*, and so on. They have singular and plural forms, which are shown by the spelling. They must be used with a determiner if they are singular:

> ***Dogs*** *ran wild in the streets.*
> ***The dog*** *is loose again.*
> *Fetch* ***a chair*** *for Sumit, will you?*
> *We've bought* ***six new chairs****.*

Uncountable nouns refer to things that we cannot count:

> *Sadia asked me for some* ***advice****.*
> *Anna gave us some more* ***information*** *about her* ***work****.*
> ***Homework*** *occupied much of Sonia's evening.*
> *Our* ***knowledge*** *of outer* ***space*** *is increasing daily.*

Uncountable nouns do not usually have a plural form. They are followed by a singular verb. They are not normally used with the indefinite article. (You cannot talk about '*an advice*' or '*a money*'.)

Mass nouns refer to substances that can be divided or measured but not counted. They do not usually have an indefinite article in front:

> ***Meat*** *is usually more expensive than* ***cheese****.*
> ***Sugar*** *is quite cheap.*

Mass nouns only take a plural in special cases, for instance when they refer to a particular type or types of the substance, or when they refer to a serving of the substance:

> *Ros brought out a tempting selection of* ***French cheeses****.*
> ***The principal sugars*** *are glucose, sucrose, and fructose.*
> ***Two teas****, please.*

Pronouns

A pronoun is a word that is used instead of a noun phrase or a noun. We use pronouns when we do not want to repeat the same noun in a sentence or paragraph:

> *Gary saw Sue so **he** asked **her** to help **him**.*
> *Costas was hungry so **he** stopped at a burger bar.*

There are seven different types of pronoun, classified according to their meaning and use.

Personal pronouns can be used as subject or object in a clause:

> ***He** gave **her** a box of chocolates.*
> ***We** saw **them** both on Friday.*
> *I can see **you**!*

Reflexive pronouns are used when the action of a verb is performed on the subject by the subject. They are obligatory with certain verbs:

> *The puppy entangled **itself** in the lead.*
> *I've just cut **myself** on a piece of glass.*

Reflexive pronouns are also used for emphasis:

> *Never mind. I'll do it **myself**.*
> *The professor **himself** did not know the answer.*

Possessive pronouns indicate ownership:

> *Give it back, it's **mine**.*
> *Perhaps it really is **theirs** after all.*

> **Tip for success**
> Note that possessive pronouns are never spelled with an apostrophe. Avoid the common mistake of writing *it's* for the possessive form. *It's* is a short form for *it is*.

Demonstrative pronouns indicate items that are near to or far from us:

__This__ is Betty's and __that__ is Peter's.
__These__ are nice. Where did you find them?

Relative pronouns are used to link a modifying clause (the part of a sentence that gives more information about a word or phrase) to a noun phrase or to a clause:

I don't know __what__ you mean.
That's the girl __who__ always comes top.

Interrogative pronouns are used to ask a question about the noun phrase they stand in for:

__What__ would you like for lunch?
__Which__ is the fresh milk?
__Who__ was responsible?

Indefinite pronouns are used for a broad range of reference when it is not necessary or not possible to use a personal pronoun:

__Everyone__ had a compass and a whistle.
__Neither__ wanted to give in and apologize.
__Much__ needs to be done.

Personal pronouns have **subject forms** (*I, you, he, she, it, we, they*) and **object forms** (*me, you, him, her, us, them*). It can sometimes be difficult to decide which to use, especially when you need to use two pronouns or a personal noun and a personal pronoun together. Here are some rules:

- If they are the joint *subject* of the verb, the subject form of the pronouns must be used:

  ***Jerry and I** are going to paint the house ourselves.*
  ***He and I** are going to paint it.*
  ***Melanie and I** are going shopping.*

> **Tip for success**
> Avoid the common mistake of saying, for example, **Jerry and me are ...**

- If they are the joint *object* of the verb, the object form of the pronouns must be used:

  *They decided to help **Jane and me**.*
  *I want to give **you and him** a present.*

> **Tip for success**
> Some people try too hard to be correct and make the mistake of saying, for example, *They decided to help Jane and I*. If you are not sure which pronoun to use, imagine you were only using one of them. You would never write '*They decided to help I.*', so if you remember that, you will choose the correct pronoun.

- The object form of pronouns must be used after prepositions:

  *Between **you and me**, I don't like this place.*
  *Wasn't that kind of **him**?*

You should follow the rules above, but in some situations the rules on subject and object pronouns are changing. In the following situations, it is now considered acceptable to use object pronouns, and using subject pronouns sounds extremely formal or old-fashioned:

- after the verb *be*.

  *I saw at once that it was **her**.*
  *I saw at once that it was **she**.* formal/old-fashioned

- after *than* in comparison with *be*.

  *Sylvia is cleverer **than me**.*
  *Sylvia is cleverer **than I**.* formal/old-fashioned

Adjectives

An adjective gives more information about a noun. Adjectives help us describe or pick out which particular thing among many is being referred to. Adjectives are sometimes called 'describing words':

a man	*a **tall** man*
their TV	*their **new, wide-screen** TV*
the cat	*the **fat, black-and-white** cat*

When there is more than one adjective, commas are often used between them, though it is common to see lists of adjectives without commas too. It is possible to use several adjectives at once, but in practice more than four is uncommon:

*a **happy young blonde German** girl*
***beautiful old English thatched** cottages*

The **comparative** form of an adjective is used to compare two people, things or states:

*Anna is **taller** than Mary, but Mary is **older**.*

The **superlative** form is used for more than two people, things, or states, where one of them has more of a quality than all the others:

*That is the **smallest** camera I have ever seen.*

There are two ways in which the comparative and superlative forms of adjectives are formed:

- You add ***-er*** (comparative) or ***-est*** (superlative) to the adjective. Adjectives with one syllable usually take these endings:

	comparative	superlative
bright	***brighter***	*the* ***brightest***
long	***longer***	*the* ***longest***
sharp	***sharper***	*the* ***sharpest***

If the word already ends in ***-e***, the ***-e*** must be left off. If a word ends in ***-y***, it usually takes ***-er*** or ***-est***, and the ***-y*** changes to ***-i***:

	comparative	superlative
wise	***wiser***	*the* ***wisest***
pretty	***prettier***	*the* ***prettiest***
weary	***wearier***	*the* ***weariest***

Tip for success
If you add ***-er*** or ***-est*** to adjectives of one syllable ending in a short vowel plus a consonant, you must double the final consonant, e.g. *bi**gg**er*, *sa**dd**est*.

- You add the word ***more*** or ***most*** in front of the adjective. Adjectives with three syllables or more use ***more*** or ***most*** in front of them:

	comparative	superlative
fortunate	***more*** *fortunate*	*the* ***most*** *fortunate*
relevant	***more*** *relevant*	*the* ***most*** *relevant*

Adjectives formed from participles (forms of verbs) use **more** or **most** as well:

	comparative	*superlative*
provoking	***more** provoking*	*the **most** provoking*
enthralled	***more** enthralled*	*the **most** enthralled*

Adjectives with two syllables (including those that already end in **-er**) can follow either pattern or sometimes both patterns. If you are doubtful about a two-syllable adjective, use the **more/most** pattern:

	comparative	*superlative*
shallow	***shallower*** or ***more** shallow*	*the **shallowest*** or *the **most** shallow*
polite	***politer*** or ***more** polite*	*the **politest*** or *the **most** polite*

A small group of irregular adjectives have quite different forms for the comparative and superlative forms:

	comparative	*superlative*
good	***better***	*the **best***
bad	***worse***	*the **worst***
far	***further***	*the **furthest***

Remember that in formal English *more* or *-er* should be used to compare two people, things or states. It is common to see the superlative in sentences such as:

Tom and Sam are both twelve, but Tom is tallest.
Which of the two sisters is most beautiful?

However, in more formal writing, it is safer to use the comparative:

Tom and Sam are both twelve, but Tom is taller.
Which of the two sisters is more beautiful?

To indicate the opposite of both the ***-er/-est*** and the ***more/most*** forms of comparison, ***less*** or ***least*** is always used:

	comparative	***superlative***
sharp	***less*** *sharp*	*the* ***least*** *sharp*
fortunate	***less*** *fortunate*	*the* ***least*** *fortunate*
interesting	***less*** *interesting*	*the* ***least*** *interesting*
involved	***less*** *involved*	*the* ***least*** *involved*

Tip for success
Never try to use *more* and *most* and the *-er/-est* endings together. It is a common mistake to write things like '*the most cleverest person*', but this is not correct English.

Adverbs

Adverbs can sometimes be difficult to identify because the term 'adverb' covers several quite different types of word. However, the basic characteristic of an adverb is that it gives information about the way that an action is carried out or when and where it takes place.

Most adverbs are formed by adding ***-ly*** to the end of the related adjective:

slow	*slowly*
clever	*cleverly*
annual	*annually*

Words which end in ***-ble*** drop the ***-e*** before ***-ly*** is added. So do the words *true* and *due*:

sensible	*sensibly*
suitable	*suitably*
true	*truly*
due	*duly*

Tip for success
A common spelling mistake is to add ***-ley***. This mistake is often made when the adjective ends in the letter ***-e***. Note the correct spelling of adverbs formed from adjectives ending in ***-e***, e.g. extreme/extremely, divine/divinely, free/freely.

Adjectives that end in ***-y*** change to ***-i*** before adding ***-ly***, unless, like *sly* or *dry*, they have only one syllable:

happy	*happily*
greedy	*greedily*
sly	*slyly*

Some adverbs keep the same spelling as the adjective to which they are related. It is often difficult to tell at first whether the word is an adjective or an adverb. The general rule is to look at the other words which it occurs with. If it comes before a noun it is probably an adjective:

*a **short way***	*a **late meeting***
*a **long pause***	*an **early lecture***

If it relates to a verb or an adjective it is probably an adverb:

*The lesson **was cut short**.*
*We **met late** at night.*
*Don't **stay long**.*
*He **came in early**.*

Sentence adverbs are used at the beginning of sentences or clauses. They can be adverbs ending in -ly or other adverbs, e.g. nevertheless, however:

***Foolishly**, I gave him my address.*
***Actually**, I don't mind.*
***Nevertheless**, we must give him an answer.*

Adverbs of degree are words like *rather*, *quite*, *too* and *almost*, and they come before adjectives or other adverbs:

*She seems **rather** nice*
*Angus is a **very** good tennis player.*
*She began to cry, **quite** loudly.*

Some **adverbs of place** have the same spelling as prepositions. However, these adverbs do not have an object, and are often found at the end of a sentence or clause:

He rushed ***in****.*
She hurried ***over****.*
The two friends fell ***out****.*

Just like adjectives, some adverbs have **comparative and superlative** forms. These are usually formed with ***more*** and ***most***:

Could you speak ***more slowly****, please?*
Mrs Kay's class behaved (the) ***most sensibly****.*

To indicate the opposite of comparatives and superlatives, ***less*** and ***least*** are used:

I checked her work a bit ***less thoroughly*** *this time.*
This product worked (the) ***least effectively****.*

Note the adverb forms of ***good*** and ***bad***:

adjective	***adverb***	***comparative adverb***	***superlative adverb***
good *bad*	*well* *badly*	*better* *worse*	*best* *worst*

Determiners

A **determiner** is used to point more precisely to the person, thing, or idea that is being talked about. Determiners make the reference of nouns more specific. If I say '***this** car*' it is clear that I mean a particular car which is near me. If I change it to '***my** car*' I am saying something quite specific about ownership.

Determiners include:

- The **indefinite article** (*a*) and the **definite article** (*the*).
- Words known as **demonstratives**, that show where something is, especially in relation to the speaker or writer: *this, that, these, those*.
- Words known as **possessives**, that show who or what something belongs to: *my, your, his, its, our, their*.
- Words known as **quantifiers**, that show the amount of something, e.g.: *some, any, few, enough, much*.
- **Cardinal numbers** (*one, two, three, etc.*) and **ordinal numbers** (*first, second, third, etc.*)
- Words known as **distributives**: *each, every, either, neither*.
- Words known as **exclamatives**, that are used in exclamations: *what, such*.

Prepositions

A preposition is one of a small but very common group of words that relate different items to each other. Most English prepositions have a number of meanings that are particular to each preposition.

Simple prepositions consist of one word, e.g. *in*, *on*, *under*. Complex prepositions consist of more than one word, e.g. *due to*, *together with*, *on top of*, *in spite of*, *out of*.

The list below shows all the common simple prepositions. Some words can be either **prepositions** or **adverbs**, depending on how they are used and what they combine with. A preposition needs an object, rather like a transitive verb. The words in *italics* are the prepositions that can also be used as **adverbs**.

> *aboard*, *about*, *above*, *across*, *after*, against, *along*, *alongside*, amid, among, *around*, as, at, atop, bar, *before*, *behind*, *below*, *beneath*, *beside*, *between*, *beyond*, *by*, despite, *down* during, for, from, *in*, *inside*, into, like, *near*, of, *off*, *on*, onto, *opposite*, *outside*, *over*, *past*, pending, per, prior, pro, re, regarding, *round*, *since*, than, *through*, *throughout*, till, to, towards, *under*, *underneath*, until, unto, *up*, upon, via, with, *within*, *without*

In modern English, it is usually considered acceptable to end a sentence with a preposition, though in very formal written English, you may want to avoid it:

> *That's the girl we were talking about.*
> (acceptable for most forms of writing)
>
> *That's the girl about whom we were talking.*
> (very formal)

Conjunctions

A **conjunction** joins two or more nouns or clauses to each other. Conjunctions are sometimes called 'joining words':

> *I went to the shop* ***and*** *bought some bread.*
> *I bought some bread,* ***but*** *I forgot to get the milk.*

In most formal writing, it is not considered good style to start a sentence with a conjunction. However, in more creative styles of writing, this is sometimes done for effect:

> *I did not expect him to give me any financial support. Or any support at all, come to that.*

Tenses

Verb forms use tense to show the time of what you are writing about, in other words whether it is in the past, the present, or the future:

> *Jessica **works** in the post office.*
> *Laurence **worked** in the post office over the Christmas holidays.*

There are two types of tense in English:

- **Simple tenses** consist of a single word.
- **Compound tenses** are formed using the present or past forms of auxiliary verbs with another verb ending in *-ing* or *-ed*.

These are the tenses in English:

Present simple

> *I/we/you/they **play***
> *he/she/it **plays***

Examples of the present simple are:

> *I **go** to college in London.*
> *Manuela **sings** in a choir.*

Past simple

> *I/we/you/they **played***
> *he/she/it **played***

Examples of the past simple are:

*I **cooked** a meal.*
*He **saw** a tiger.*

Future simple

*I/we/you/they **will play***
*he/she/it **will play***

Examples of the future simple are:

*We **will give** you the money.*
*Louis **will phone** you later.*

Present Perfect

*I/we/you/they **have played***
*he/she/it **has played***

Examples of the present perfect are:

*I **have ordered** a new sofa.*
*This illness **has ruined** my life.*

Past Perfect

*I/we/you/they **had played***
*he/she/it **had played***

Examples of the past perfect are:

*They **had noticed** a strange smell.*
*She **had visited** Paris before.*

Future Perfect

I/we/you/they ***will have played***
he/she/it ***will have played***

Examples of the future perfect are:

We ***will have finished*** *before dark.*
Gerry ***will have done*** *his work by then.*

Present Continuous

I am playing
we/you/they ***are playing***
he/she/it ***is playing***

Examples of the present continuous are:

I ***am waiting*** *for Jack.*
She ***is finishing*** *her meal.*

Past Continuous

I ***was playing***
we/you/they ***were playing***
he/she/it ***was playing***

Examples of the past continuous are:

We ***were trying*** *to see the queen.*
The water ***was splashing*** *all over the floor.*

Tip for success
Be sure to use the correct form of the auxiliary verb.
It is not correct to write '*We was trying ...*'.

Future continuous

I/we/you/they ***will be playing***
he/she/it ***will be playing***

Examples of the future continuous are:

Our choir ***will be performing*** *in the cathedral.*
Mum ***will be worrying*** *about us.*

Present Perfect Continuous

I/we/you/they ***have been playing***
he/she/it ***has been playing***

Examples of the present perfect continuous are:

We ***have been trying*** *to phone you all morning.*
The snow ***has been falling*** *all night.*

Past Perfect Continuous

I/we/you/they ***had been playing***
he/she/it ***had been playing***

Examples of the past perfect continuous are:

The children ***had been using*** *my computer.*
Anna ***had been sitting*** *there all day.*

Future Perfect Continuous

I/we/you/they ***will have been playing***
he/she/it ***will have been playing***

Examples of the future perfect continuous are:

> *On Sunday, we **will have been living** here for 10 years.*
> *I **will have been working** on the project for over a year.*

Regular and irregular verbs

Regular verbs form their past tenses with *-ed*:

> *She wait**ed** for me.*
> *I look**ed** but I couldn't see her.*

However, there are many common verbs that form their past tenses in a different way. Many of these have a different form for their simple past tenses and their compound past tenses. If you are not sure of the past form of a verb, check in a dictionary: the irregular ones will be shown.

Some examples of common verbs with irregular past forms are:

> *become > became > become*
> *blow > blew > blown*
> *cost > cost > cost*
> *go > went > been*
> *leave > left > left*
> *swim > swam > swum*
> *take > took > taken*

Subject, object and indirect object

The **subject** of a sentence is the person or thing that does the verb. The subject can be a noun, a noun phrase or a pronoun:

> ***Adam*** *played the piano.*
> ***The man in the red coat*** *asked me some questions.*
> ***Her car*** *broke down.*
> ***They*** *forgot to buy any milk.*

All sentences must have a subject.

The **object** of a sentence usually comes after the verb. It can also be a noun, a noun phrase or a pronoun.

> *I spilled* ***the milk****.*
> *She saw* ***a large, black bird****.*
> *We were able to fix* ***the broken shelf****.*
> *I couldn't find* ***it****.*

Not all sentences have an object:

> *She was riding.* (no object)
> *She was riding a horse.* (with object)
> *Erica was writing.* (no object)
> *Erica was writing a letter.* (with object)

Some verbs also have another sort of object, called an **indirect object**. An indirect object names the person for or to whom something is done. It is usually needed with verbs like *give*, *find* and *owe*:

> *Mike owes Tom* ***five pounds****.*
> *Naveen gave me* ***a box of chocolates****.*
> *Susan bought her rabbit* ***some more food****.*

Agreement

Agreement means making sure that all the words and phrases in a sentence have the correct form in relation to one another.

Subject/verb agreement

The form of the verb must be the correct one to go with the subject:

The house is very large. (singular subject, singular verb)

The stars are very bright. (plural subject, plural verb)

In very long sentences, if can be easy to make a mistake, especially if the verb is a long way from the subject.

If two singular subjects are joined by *and*, they need a plural verb:

Parminder and Amandeep ***are*** *going on holiday.*
The table and the desk ***need*** *polishing.*

However, if the two things joined with *and* are thought of as one thing, a singular verb is used:

Fish and chips ***is*** *my favourite meal.*
Bed and breakfast ***is*** *the cheapest form of accommodation.*

If the subject has *each*, *every*, or *no* before it, the verb should be singular, and the same is true for *any* before a singular subject:

Every seat ***was*** *taken already.*
Each vase ***holds*** *four or five roses.*

If two singular subjects are joined by *or*, *nor*, *neither/nor*, *either/or* or *not only/but also*, a singular verb is used:

Neither Blake nor Jones ***was*** *available for comment.*
Either Mrs Spiers or Mr Turner ***takes*** *the children to football.*

Titles of books, films, songs, etc. have a singular verb even if the title itself is plural:

'The Birds' is a really scary film.
'Daffodils' was the first poem I learned at school.

Pronoun agreement

Pronouns must have the correct form in relation to the things they refer to. Pronouns often refer back to another sentence:

The car *started fine, but* ***it*** *broke down half way to Manchester.*
I asked ***Adam and Ella*** *to tidy their rooms. When* ***they*** *had finished, we went bowling.*

Singular subject followed by plural pronoun

Look at this sentence:

Any pupil who is going on the school trip should hand in their payment at the office.

In this sentence, *any pupil* is singular, and the verb is is singular, but the plural pronoun *their* has been used.

Some people who have very strict rules on grammar would consider this to be wrong. However, this use of plural pronouns is widely accepted in modern English, especially because it allows us to avoid the clumsy use of *he/she* or *he* or *she*. It is safe to use in all but the most formal of documents.

Agreement with group nouns

Group nouns are words like *committee* or *parliament*, which can mean the group or all the individuals in it.

In British English, you can use either a singular or a plural verb with these nouns, but be sure to be consistent:

> *The army* ***was*** *marching towards us.*
> *The army* ***were*** *marching towards us.*

In American English, the singular form of the verb is used with group nouns.

Tense agreement

You must make sure that the tenses you use in a sentence or paragraph relate correctly to each other:

> *While I was waiting, I* ***seen*** *a film.* (incorrect)
> *While I was waiting, I* ***saw*** *a film.* (correct)
>
> *By midday, I* ***answered*** *over 50 letters.* (incorrect)
> *By midday, I* ***had answered*** *over 50 letters.* (correct)

Be particularly careful when you use two or more modal or auxiliary verbs together. It is common to hear sentences such as:

> ***I can*** *and* ***I have done it***.

This is incorrect because *can* cannot be used with *done*. The sentence should be:

> ***I can do it*** *and* ***I have done it***.

Punctuation

The apostrophe (')

Misusing or omitting the apostrophe is one of the commonest punctuation errors.

Showing possession

The apostrophe (') is used to show that something belongs to someone. It is usually added to the end of a word and followed by an *-s*.

's is added to the end of singular words:

*a baby'**s** pushchair*
*Hannah'**s** book*
*a child'**s** cry*

's is added to the end of plural words not ending in *-s*:

*children'**s** games*
*women'**s** clothes*
*people'**s** lives*

An apostrophe alone (') is added to plural words ending in *-s*:

*Your grandparents are your parents**'** parents.*
*We're campaigning for workers**'** rights.*
*They've hired a new ladies**'** fashion guru.*

's is added to the end of names and singular words ending in *-s*:

*James'**s** car*
*the octopus'**s** tentacles*

However, an apostrophe only is often also used, especially for more formal contexts:

Dickens' novels
St Giles' Cathedral

's is added to the end of certain professions or occupations to indicate workplaces:

*She's on her way to the doctor***'s**.
*James is at the hairdresser***'s**.

's is added to the end of people or their names to indicate that you are talking about their home:

*I'm going over to Harry***'s** *for tea tonight.*
*I popped round to Mum***'s** *this afternoon, but she wasn't in.*

's can also be added to:

- whole phrases:

*My next-door neighbour***'s** *dog was barking away like mad.*
*John and Cath***'s** *house was on TV last night.*

- indefinite pronouns such as somebody or anywhere:

*Is this anybody***'s** *pencil case?*
*It's nobody***'s** *fault but mine.*

- each other:

*We're getting used to each other***'s** *habits.*
*We kept forgetting each other***'s** *names.*

When the possessor is an inanimate object (rather than a living thing), the apostrophe is not used and the word order is changed:

> *the middle of the street* (not *the street's middle*)
> *the front of the house* (not *the house's front*)

To test whether an apostrophe is in the right place, think about who the owner is:

> *the boy**'s** books* (= the books belonging to the boy)
> *the boy**s'** books* (= the books belonging to the boys)

> **Key points to remember**
> An apostrophe is *not* used to form possessive pronouns such as *its*, *yours*, or *theirs*.
>
> An apostrophe is *not* used to form the plurals of words such as *potatoes* or *tomatoes*.

With letters and numbers

An apostrophe is used in front of two figures referring to a year or decade:

> *French students rioted in **'68** [short for '1968'].*
> *He worked as a schoolteacher during the **'60s** and early **'90s**.*

An apostrophe can be used in plurals of letters and numbers to make them more readable:

> *Mind your p**'s** and q**'s**.*
> *His 2**'s** look a bit like 7**'s**.*
> *She got straight A**'s** in her exams.*

Key point to remember
it's = it is, e.g. *It's a holiday today.*
its = belonging to it, e.g. *The dog was scratching its ear.*

Contracted forms

An apostrophe is used in shortened forms of words to show that one or more letters have been missed out. Contractions are usually shortened forms of auxiliary verbs:

be	**have**
*I'**m***	*I/we/they'**ve*** *(have)*
*We/you/they'**re*** *(are)*	*He/she/it/one'**s*** *(has)*
*He/she/it/one'**s*** *(is)*	*I/we/you/he/she/it/one/they'**d*** *(had)*

would
*I/we/you/he/she/it/one/they'**d*** *(would)*

or the negative not:

not
*We/you/they are**n't***
*He/she/it/one is**n't***
*I/we/they have**n't***
*He/she/it/one has**n't***

In order to work out what the contracted forms ***'s*** and ***'d*** represent, you need to look at what follows it:

If ***'s*** is followed by an *-ing* form, it represents the auxiliary *is*.

*She**'s reading** a book about the ancient Egyptians.*
*He**'s going** to Ibiza for his holidays.*

If **'s** is followed by an adjective or a noun phrase, it represents the main verb **is**:

> *She**'s nervous** about meeting my parents.*
> *He**'s brilliant** at maths.*

If **'s** is followed by a past participle, it can represent *is* as it is used in the passive:

> *He**'s portrayed** by the media as a kindly old grandfather.*
> *It**'s** often **said** that rock stars are frustrated actors.*

or *has* as it is used in the present perfect:

> *She**'s broken** her wrist.*
> *It**'s been** ages since we last saw you.*

If **'s** is followed by *got*, it represents the auxiliary *has*:

> *She**'s got** two brothers and one sister.*
> *It**'s got** everything you could want.*

If **'d** is followed by a past participle, it represents the auxiliary *had*:

> *I**'d raced** against him before, but never in a marathon.*
> *She couldn't believe what she**'d done**.*

If **'d** is followed by a base form, it represents the modal auxiliary *would*:

> *I**'d give up** now, if I were you.*
> *When we were kids we**'d spend** hours out on our bikes.*

If **'d** is followed by *rather* or *better*, it represents the modal auxiliary would:

> *We**'d better** go home soon.*
> *I**'d rather** not talk about that.*

The comma (,)

The comma marks a short pause between parts of a sentence.

Separating main clauses

Main clauses (main parts of sentences) that are joined together with *and* or *but* do not normally have a comma before the conjunction unless the two clauses have different subjects:

You go out of the door and turn immediately left.
It was cold outside, but we decided to go out for a walk anyway.

Separating subordinate clauses from main clauses

Commas are normally used if the subordinate clause (the part of the sentence that is not the main part) comes before the main clause:

If you have any problems, just call me.
Just call me if you have any problems.

Sometimes a comma is used even when the main clause comes first, if the clauses are particularly long:

We should be able to finish the work by the end of the week,
if nothing unexpected turns up between now and then.

Separating relative clauses from main clauses

Commas are used to mark off non-defining relative clauses. This is the type of clause that adds to information about a noun or noun phrase:

> *My next-door neighbour, who works from home, is keeping an eye on the house while we're away.*
>
> *She moved to Los Angeles, where she was immediately signed as a singer songwriter.*

Commas are not required in defining relative clauses (clauses that say who or what something is):

> *Let's make sure the money goes to the people* ***who need it most****.*
> *The computer* ***(that) I borrowed*** *kept on crashing.*

Separating items in a list

Commas are used to separate three or more items in a list or series:

> *She got out bread**,** butter**,** and jam.*

Note that the comma is often not given before the final *and* or *or*:

> *They breed dogs**,** cats**,** rabbits and hamsters.*
> *We did canoeing**,** climbing and archery.*

Separating adjectives

Commas are often used between adjectives, whether they come before the noun or after a linking verb:

> *It was a hot, dry and dusty road.*
> *It's wet, cold and windy outside.*

A comma is not usually used before an adjective that is followed by *and*.

With adverbials

When an adverbial such as *however*, *therefore* or *unfortunately* refers to a whole sentence, it is separated from the rest of the sentence by a comma:

> *However, police would not confirm this rumour.*
> *Therefore, I try to avoid using the car as much as possible.*

With question tags and short answers

Commas are used before question tags and after *yes* or *no* in short answers:

> *It's quite cold today, isn't it?*
> *He's up to date with all his injections, isn't he?*
> *Are you the mother of these children? – Yes, I am.*
> *You're Amy Osborne, aren't you? – No, I'm not.*

With names

Commas are used to separate the name of a person or group being spoken to from the rest of the sentence:

> *And now, ladies and gentlemen, please raise your glasses in a toast to the happy couple.*
> *Come on, Olivia, be reasonable.*
> *Dad, can you come and help me, please?*

With discourse markers

Commas are used to separate discourse markers (spoken phrases, often with little meaning, that people use before or between parts of sentences) from the rest of the sentence:

> *Well, believe it or not, I actually passed!*
> *Now then, let's see what's on TV tonight.*
> *Actually, I quite enjoyed it.*

In reported speech

Commas are used to follow direct speech (if there is no question or exclamation mark after the quotation), or to show that it comes next:

> *'I don't understand this question,' said Peter.*
> *Peter said, 'I don't understand this question.'*
> *'You're crazy!' Claire exclaimed.*
> *'What do you think you're doing?' Dad bellowed.*

It is also possible to punctuate reported speech of the type *Peter said*, '...' using a colon instead of a comma. This is a particularly common practice in American English:

Peter said: 'Dream on.'

In dates

A comma must be used between the day of the month and the year, when the two numbers are next to each other:

March 31, 2011

Quotation marks (' ') or (" ")

Direct speech

Direct speech gives the actual words that a speaker used. It is common in novels and other writing where the words of a speaker are quoted.

The words spoken are enclosed in single or double quotation marks:

> ***'Have you been to the new shopping precinct yet?'*** *enquired Shona.*
> ***'I've already seen it,'*** *John replied.*

The comma comes inside the quotation marks, unless the reporting verb is positioned inside a reported sentence that itself does not require a comma:

> *'There is'*, *Monica said*, *'nothing we can do about it.'*

Other uses

Single quotation marks are sometimes used:

- to draw attention to a word

> *The word **'book'** can be used as a noun or a verb.*

> *Verbs such as **'criticize'** can be spelled with an 's' or a 'z'.*

- to indicate an unusual use of a word

  *She pointed out that websites used for internet voting could be **'spoofed'**.*

  *You could go to one of those parties where you swap (or **'swish'**) clothes.*

- to suggest that the writer wants to be distanced from a word.

  *I think he's too mean to go away on holiday, but he insists on calling it a **'staycation'**.*

  *I keep reading about **'coatigans'** in fashion magazines.*

Note that the full stop comes after the quotation marks in such cases.

Capital letters

A capital (or 'upper case') letter is used to mark the beginning of a sentence.

When I was 20, I dropped out of university and became a model.

Capital letters are also used for the first letter in proper nouns. These include:

- people's names

  Jenny Forbes *William Davidson*

- days of the week

  Wednesday *Saturday*

- months of the year

  August *January*

- public holidays

  Christmas *Yom Kippur*

- nationalities

  Spanish *Iraqi*

- languages

  Swahili *Flemish*

- geographical locations

***A**ustralia*	***L**och **N**ess*
***M**ount **E**verest*	***T**he **M**editerranean **S**ea*

- company names

***D**yson*	***H**arper**C**ollins*

- religions

***I**slam*	***B**uddhism*

Capital letters are also used for the first letter in titles of books, magazines, newspapers, TV shows, films, etc. Where there are several words, a capital letter is usually used for all the main content words in the title (i.e. not the prepositions or the determiners – unless they are the first word in the title).

***T**he **T**imes*	***H**ello!*
***T**welfth **N**ight*	***T**he **S**ecret **G**arden*
***N**ewsnight*	***M**amma **M**ia!*

The full stop (.)

Full stops are used:

- to mark the end of a sentence

  Let's have some lunch.
  I have to catch a bus in ten minutes.

- to mark the end of a sentence fragment

  Are you cold? – Yes, a bit.
  Do you like this sort of music? Not really.

- in initials for people's names, although this practice is becoming less frequent

J.K. Rowling	*Iain M. Banks*
M.C. Hammer	*Ronald G. Hardie*

- after abbreviations, although this practice is becoming less frequent

  P.S. Do pop in next time you're passing.
  She's moved to the I.T. department.
  R.S.V.P. to Helen Douglas on 01234 676240.
  The U.S. government reacted strongly to the accusation.

When an abbreviation consists of a shortened word such as *Re.* or *Prof.*, a full stop is needed.

Re. your suggestion that we shorten the lunch hour, could we arrange a quick meeting to discuss the various options?
Prof. John Johansson will be speaking on the subject of 'Discourse in the Electronic Age'.
Flight BA 345: dep. 09.44 arr. 11.10.

When an abbreviation contains the last letter of the shortened word, a full stop is not needed.

Dr *McDonald*	**St** *Mary's School*
41, Douglas **Rd**	*Universal Pictures (UK)* **Ltd**

Note that full stops are not used in many common sets of initials:

Did you see that programme on **BBC** *4 last night?*
Millions of people now call the **NHS** *Direct helpline each year.*

or at the end of headlines, headings and titles:

Fear grips global stock markets
Teaching grammar as a liberating force
Wuthering Heights

Remember that a full stop, and not a question mark, is used after an indirect question or a polite request:

He asked if the bus had left.
Will you open your books on page 14.
I wonder what's happened.
She asked him where he was going.

In American English, the full stop is called a period.

The question mark (?)

The question mark marks the end of a question:

When will we be arriving?
Why did you do that?
Does any of this matter?
He's certain to be elected, isn't he?

Question marks are used in direct questions, i.e. when the actual words of a speaker are used. A reported question should end with a full stop:

The lady said, 'Where are you going?'
The lady asked where she was going.

Note that you put a question mark at the end of a question, even if the words in the sentence are not in the normal question order, or some words are omitted. Care is needed here as such a sentence can look, at first sight, like a statement rather than a question:

You know he doesn't live here any longer?

A full stop, rather than a question mark, is used after an indirect question:

I'd like to know what you've been doing all this time.
I wonder what's happened.

A full stop also replaces a question mark at the end of a sentence which looks like a question if, in fact, it is really a polite request:

Will you please return the completed forms to me.
Would you please call my brother and ask him to collect my car.

The exclamation mark (!)

The exclamation mark is used after exclamations and emphatic expressions:

I can't believe it!
Oh, no! Look at this mess!

Tip for success
The exclamation mark loses its effect if it is overused. It is better to use a full stop after a sentence expressing mild excitement or humour.

It was such a beautiful day.
I felt like such a fool.

The colon (:)

The colon indicates a break between two main clauses which is stronger than a comma but weaker than a full stop.

A colon is used:

- in front of a list

  I used three colours: green, blue and pink.
  Make sure you wear clothes made from natural fibres: cotton, silk and wool.

- in front of an explanation or a reason

  Nevertheless, the main problem remained: what should be done with the two men?
  I decided against going away this weekend: the weather forecast was dreadful.

- after introductory headings

  Cooking time: about five minutes.
  Start time: 10 o'clock.

- in more formal writing, between two main clauses that are connected

  It made me feel claustrophobic: what, I wonder, would happen to someone who was really unable to tolerate being locked into such a tiny space?
  Be patient: the next book in the series has not yet been published.

- in front of the second part of a book title

  Farming and wildlife: a study in compromise
  Beyond single words: the most frequent collocations in spoken English

- to introduce direct speech, especially in American English, or when the quotation is particularly long

  He said: 'You owe me three dollars and twenty-five cents.'
  The Health Minister said: 'The NHS IT programme will mean that patients will get access to more comprehensive information to help them make choices.'

The semicolon (;)

The semicolon is used to mark a break between two main clauses when there is a balance or a contrast between the clauses.

Compare:

> *The engine roared into life. The propellers began to turn. The plane taxied down the runway ready for takeoff.*

with:

> *The engine roared into life; the propellers began to turn; the plane taxied down the runway ready for takeoff.*

A useful test to work out when to use a semicolon is to ask yourself whether the two clauses could be written instead as separate sentences. If the answer is 'yes', then you can use a semicolon.

Note that it is quite acceptable to use a full stop in these cases, but a semicolon is preferable if you wish to convey the sense of a link or continuity between the parts of your sentence:

> *I'm not that interested in jazz; I prefer classical music.*
> *He knew everything about me; I had never even heard of him.*

A semicolon is also used to separate items in a list, especially if the listed items are phrases or clauses, which may already contain commas:

> *The holiday was a disaster: the flight was four hours late; the hotel, which was described as 'luxury', was dirty; and it rained for the whole fortnight.*

Brackets ( )

Brackets (also called parentheses) are used to enclose a word or words which can be left out and still leave a meaningful sentence:

> *The wooded area* **(***see map below***)** *is approximately 4,000 hectares.*
> *This is a process which Hayek* **(***a writer who came to rather different conclusions***)** *also observed.*

Brackets are also used to show alternatives or options:

> *Any student***(***s***)** *interested in taking part should email me.*
> *A goat should give from three to six pints* **(***1.7 to 3.4 litres***)** *of milk a day.*

Note that when the structure of the sentence as a whole demands punctuation after a bracketed section, the punctuation is given outside the brackets:

> *I haven't yet spoken to John* **(***I mean John Maple, my boss***),** *but I have a meeting with him on Friday.*
> *For lunch we had sandwiches* **(***pastrami on rye and so on***),** *salami, coleslaw, fried chicken, and potato salad.*

Punctuation is given before the closing brackets only when it applies to the bracketed section rather than to the sentence as a whole:

> *He's very handsome* **(***positively gorgeous in fact!***)** *and still single.*

Square brackets [ ]

Square brackets are used, usually in books and articles, when supplying words that make a quotation clearer or that comment on it, although they were not originally said or written:

> *Mr Runcie concluded: 'The novel is at its strongest when describing the dignity of Cambridge* **[***a slave***]** *and the education of Emily* **[***the daughter of an absentee landlord***]***.'*

Square brackets with dots are used to show where some words have been missed out:

> *Greg Smith, chief executive of Pharm-wise* **[...]***, addressed the meeting.*

The hyphen (-)

The hyphen joins words or parts of words.

Hyphens are used at the ends of lines where a word has been split, to warn the reader that the word continues on the next line. If the word you need to split is clearly made up of two or more smaller words or elements, you should put the hyphen after the first of these parts. Otherwise, you put the hyphen at the end of a syllable:

wheel-barrow	*inter-national*
listen-ing	*compli-mentary*
infor-mation	

It is best not to add a hyphen if the word is a short one, or if it would mean writing just one or two letters at the end or beginning of a line. For example, it would be better to write 'unnatural' on the line below, rather than writing 'un-' on one line and 'natural' on the next.

Prefixes that are used in front of a word beginning with a capital letter always have a hyphen after them:

a wave of anti-British feeling
a neo-Byzantine cathedral

A hyphen is used to join two or more words that together form an adjective, where this adjective is used before the noun it describes:

an up-to-date account
a last-minute rush
a six-year-old boy

The hyphen is omitted when the adjective so formed comes after the noun or pronoun it describes:

The accounts are up to date.
It was all rather last minute.
He's six years old.

Some common compound nouns are usually written with hyphens:

mother-in-law *great-grandmother*

Hyphens can be used to split words that have been formed by adding a prefix to another word, especially to avoid an awkward combination of letters or confusion with another word:

re-elect
re-covering furniture
re-creation

The dash (–)

A spaced dash (i.e. with a single space before and after it) is used:

- at the beginning and end of a comment that interrupts the flow of a sentence

  Now children – Kenneth, stop that immediately! – open your books on page 20.

- to separate off extra information

  Boots and shoes – all shapes, sizes and colours – tumbled out.

An unspaced dash (i.e. with no space before or after it) is used:

- to indicate a range

  pages 26–42

- between two adjectives or noun modifiers (nouns that go before other nouns) that indicate that two countries or groups are involved in something or that an individual has two roles or aspects

  Swedish–Norwegian relations improved,
  the United States–Canada free trade pact
  a mathematician–philosopher

- to indicate that something such as a plane or a train goes between two places

  the Anguilla–St Kitts flight
  the New York–Montreal train

The slash (/)

The slash separates letters, words or numbers. It is used to indicate alternatives, ratios and ranges, and in website addresses:

he/she/it
200 km/hr
the 2001/02 accounting year
http://www.abcdefg.com

Spelling

Why is spelling important?

Spelling in English is certainly not easy. Unlike with many other languages, it is often difficult to guess spellings from the way a word sounds.

However, learning to spell well is important for good communication, and will help you with:

- **understanding other people**. If you are a confident speller, you will be able to read and understand written material easily and efficiently. Reading will probably be more fun, so you will read more. As a result, your reading, spelling and writing are likely to improve.

- **making yourself understood**. If your writing is full of spelling mistakes, other people may find it hard to understand what you are trying to say. If a word is spelled incorrectly, they may struggle to work out which word you meant. If you are trying to persuade them to take your side in an argument, it may be more difficult to convince them. Poor spelling makes a piece of written work less appealing and less effective.

Whether we like it or not, other people judge us on the way we write. Although some people believe that spelling is not important and are not put off by mistakes in a piece of writing, many (if not most) people think that good spelling does matter.

Ways to improve your spelling

A good way to learn spellings is to use the 'Look, Say, Cover, Write, Check' method:

- **Look** at the word carefully.
- **Say** the word aloud to yourself, listening to how it sounds.
- **Cover** the word and try to remember what it looks like.
- **Write** the word.
- **Check** what you have written to see if you have got it right.

Try **breaking the word up into its syllables** and sound them out, pronouncing even the silent letters:

> **dictionary** = dic + tion + ar + y
> **Wednesday** = Wed + nes + day
> **handkerchief** = hand + ker + chief
> **business** = bus + i + ness

Look for patterns and relations between words. If there is a word you do not know how to spell, try to think of another word that is related to it, e.g. succeed/successful, govern/government.

Write words down to see if they 'look right'. Often, if you write down 2 possible versions of a word, you will know which one is correct.

Read a lot. The more you read, the better you will become at noticing when a word is spelled wrongly.

Suffixes and prefixes

Suffixes are parts of words that are added to the end of a base word to make another word in that family, e.g. dark + ness = darkness, happy + ly = happily. Prefixes are added to the beginning of words, e.g. dis- + like = dislike, inter- + national = international.

There are several useful rules about adding suffixes and prefixes:

Adding a suffix to words that end with a silent *e*:
When you add a suffix that begins with a vowel, you drop the **e**:

> *abbreviat**e** + -ion = abbreviation*
> *desir**e** + -able = desirable*
> *hop**e** + -ing = hoping*

Be careful, though. If the word ends in **ce** and sounds like **s**, or the word ends in **ge** and sounds like **j**, you do not drop the final **e**:

> *noti**ce** + -able = noticeable*
> *chan**ge** + -able = changeable*
> *outra**ge** + -ous = outrageous*

Adding a suffix to words that end with a consonant
In words of one syllable ending in a short vowel plus a consonant, you double the final consonant when you add a suffix that begins with a vowel:

> *run + -ing = ru**nn**ing*
> *thin + -est = thi**nn**est*
> *swim + -er = swi**mm**er*

In words of more than one syllable ending in a single vowel plus a consonant, if the stress is on the end of the word when it is pronounced, you double the final consonant when you add a suffix that begins with a vowel:

> *begin + ing = begi**nn**ing*
> *commit + -ed = commi**tt**ed*
> *occur + -ence = occu**rr**ence*

When you add a suffix that begins with a vowel to a word that ends in a single vowel plus **l** or **p**, you double the **l** or **p**:

> *cancel + -ation = cance**ll**ation*
> *travel + -er = trave**ll**er*
> *kidnap + -er = kidna**pp**er*
> *wrap + -ing = wra**pp**ing*

(Note that in American English, the **l** is not usually doubled.)

When you add a suffix that begins with **e**, **i** or **y** to a word that ends in **c**, you add a **k** after the **c**. This is to keep the hard **k** sound when it is pronounced:

> *mimic + -ed = mimi**ck**ed*
> *picnic + ing = picni**ck**ing*
> *panic + -y = pani**ck**y*

Adding a suffix to words that end with *our*
When you add the suffixes **-ous** or **-ary** to a word that ends with **-our** you drop the **u** from **our**:

> *glamour + -ous = glam**o**rous*
> *humour + -ous = hum**o**rous*
> *honour + -able = hon**o**rary*

Adding a suffix to words that end with *y*

When you add a suffix to a word that ends with a consonant plus **y**, you change the **y** to **i**:

beauty + -ful = beautiful
crazy + -ly = crazily
happy + -ness = happiness

Be careful though, there are a few words that do not follow this rule. The most common one is 'shy':

shy + **-ly** *= shyly*

Adding the *ly* suffix to words that end with *le*:

When you make an adverb by adding the suffix **-ly** to an adjective that ends with **le**, you drop the **le** from the adjective:

gentle + **-ly** *= gently*
idle + **-ly** *= idly*
subtle + **-ly** *= subtly*
regrettable + **ly** *= regrettably*
arguable + **ly** *= arguably*

Tip for success

There are only three verbs in English that end in -ceed: *succeed, proceed, exceed*. All the others with that sound end in -cede, except the one English verb that ends in -sede: *supersede*.

Words ending in *ful*:
You always spell the suffix **ful** with just one **l**, e.g:

beautiful, faithful, grateful, hopeful, painful, cupful

Words beginning with *al*:
When **all** and another word are joined to make a word without a hyphen, you drop the second **l**, e.g.:

all + ready = already
all + though = although
all + together = altogether

Forming plurals

Making plurals of words that end with a consonant followed by *y*:
When you make a plural of a word that ends with a consonant plus **y**, you change the **y** to **i** and add **-es**:

> *fair**y** + -es = fair**ies***
> *qualit**y** + -es = qualit**ies***
> *stor**y** + -es = stor**ies***

Making plurals of words that end with a vowel followed by *y*:
When you make a plural of a word that ends with a vowel plus **y**, you add **-s**:

> *bo**y** + -s = boys*
> *da**y** + -s = days*
> *donke**y** + -s = donkeys*

Making plurals of words that end with *s*, *x*, *z*, *sh* or *ch*
When you make a plural of a word that ends with **s**, **x**, **z**, **sh** or **ch**, you add **-es**:

> *bus + -es = buses*
> *fox + -es = foxes*
> *match + -es = matches*

Making plurals of words that end with *eau*:
Words that end with **eau** are French words that have come into English, and you make their plurals by adding **-x** or **-s**. The **-x** ending is the French one, and the **-s** ending is the English one. Both forms are acceptable for these words:

> *bureau + -x = bureaux, bureau + -s = bureaus*
> *gateau + -x = gateaux, gateau + -s = gateaus*

Making plurals of words that end with a single *o*
When you make the plural of a word that ends with a single **o**, you add **-s**:

memo + -s = memos
solo + -s = solos
zero + -s = zeros

Be careful though, there are a few words that do not follow this rule. If you have any doubt, check in your dictionary:

echo + -es = echoes
hero + -es = heroes
potato + -es = potatoes
tomato + -es = tomatoes

Making plurals of words that end with *f* or *fe*:
When you make the plural of a word that ends with **f** or **fe**, you often have to change the **f** to **v**:

leaf, *plural* leaves
life, *plural* lives
knife, *plural* knives
loaf, *plural* loaves

Be careful though, there are a few words that do not follow this rule. If you have any doubt, check in your dictionary:

roof, *plural* roofs

Irregular plurals
Some plurals do not follow any of the usual rules. You just have to learn them, or check in your dictionary if you are not sure.

Some words do not change at all in the plural:

sheep, *plural* sheep
aircraft, *plural* aircraft
species, *plural* species

Some change in other ways:

foot, *plural* feet
mouse, *plural* mice
analysis, *plural* analyses
phenomenon, *plural* phenomena
child, *plural* children

Compound words (words made of two or more words put together) follow the same pattern as that of their last part:

grandchild, *plural* grandchildren

Alternative plurals
Some plurals have more than one possible form. Often one form is more formal or technical than the other, so you will want to think about the context in which you are using it. For example, you might use the more technical plurals in a scientific context.

formula, *plural* formulas or (technical) formulae
fungus, *plural* funguses or (technical) fungi

-ise or -ize?

The question of whether a verb should end in **-ise** or **-ize** is one that people argue about. Historically, both endings have always been used in English.

The **-ize** spelling has been preferred in American English for over a century, and this has led some people to think that **-ize** is an Americanism, and object to its use in British English.

Collins Dictionaries (and all other leading British dictionary publishers) show **-ize** as the main spelling form for these verbs, and **-ization** and **-izer** as the preferred forms of their derivatives (e.g. organization, organizer). It is perfectly correct also to use **-ise**, **-isation** and **-iser**. The most important thing is to keep to one style.

Be careful though – some words are *always* spelled with **-ise**:

advertise	devise	prise (meaning 'to force open')
advise	disguise	revise
chastise	excise	supervise
comprise	exercise	surprise
compromise	franchise	televise
despise	improvise	

And a few words are *always* spelled with **-ize**:

capsize	prize (meaning 'to value highly')

i before e except after c

This is a useful phrase to learn. It means that when **i** and **e** are put together to make the sound 'ee', the **i** comes before the **e**:

achieve	field	relief
brief	hygiene	siege
chief	niece	thief

However, when they follow the letter **c** in a word, the **e** comes before the **i**:

ceiling	deceit	receipt
conceive	deceive	receive

There are a few words that do not follow this rule:

caffeine	protein	seize

Silent letters

Some words contain letters that you do not pronounce, but it is still important to write them correctly, e.g.:

*lam**b***	*sig**n***	*autum**n***

Some words that begin with 'ch' are pronounced 'c':

*c**h**aracter*	*C**h**ristian*	*c**h**emical*

Words that begin with 'kn' are pronounced 'n':

***k**nee*	***k**nife*	***k**nock*

Words that begin with 'ps' are pronounced 's':

***p**sychology*	***p**seudonym*	***p**sychopath*

Some words that begin with 'sc' are pronounced 's':

*s**c**ene*	*s**c**ent*	*s**c**ientist*

Some words that begin with 'wh' are pronounced 'w' in English (but not Scottish or some American) accents:

*w**h**eel*	*w**h**ere*	*w**h**ite*

Some words begin with 'wr' and are pronounced 'r':

***w**rite*	***w**rap*	***w**rong*

Contractions

Contractions are when two or more words are put together, but part of at least one of the words is missing:

> don't = do not
> I'd = I would

We use an apostrophe to represent the missing letter or letters.

The most common contractions are of:

- **the verb** *be*:

  I'm, you're, he's, she's, it's, we're, they're

- **the verb** *have*:

  I've, you've, he's, she's, it's, we've, they've

- **the modal verb** *would*

  I'd, you'd, he'd, she'd, it'd, we'd, they'd

- **the negative** *not***, e.g.:**

  I can't
  we aren't
  they haven't
  she wouldn't

Common mistakes and controversial issues

Words that are often confused

Homophones

Homophones are words which sound the same but are spelled differently, and it is easy to become confused by them:

affect Affect is a *verb*: *How will this new law affect me?*	***effect*** Effect is a *noun*: *What will the effect of the new law be?*
already Already is an *adverb*. If something has already happened, it has happened before the present time: *I've already called an ambulance.*	***all ready*** In the phrase 'all ready', 'all' is a *quantifier* meaning the whole of a group or a thing, and ready is an *adjective*: *Are you all ready to go?*
alter Alter is a verb, meaning 'to change': *Nothing in the house had altered since 1960.*	***altar*** An altar is the holy table in a church: *The priest stood in front of the altar.*
anyone Anyone is a pronoun and always refers to people: *Has anyone seen my hat?*	***any one*** In the phrase 'any one', 'one' is a pronoun or a determiner that can refer to a person or a thing, depending on the context: *We never spend long in any one place.* *It could have happened to any one of us.*
bare Bare is an adjective meaning 'not covered' or 'not wearing any clothes': *We ran along the beach with bare feet.*	***bear*** A bear is a wild animal: *There are bears in the woods.*

board A board is a flat piece of wood: *They nailed a board over the window.*	***bored*** If you are bored, you are not interested by something: *I was so bored at school today.*
coarse Coarse is an *adjective* meaning 'having a rough texture' or 'talking and behaving in a rude way': *The sand was very coarse.* *His manners are coarse.*	***course*** Course is a *noun* with several meanings, including 'a series of lessons' and 'a route or path': *The plane changed course.* *I did a course in art history.*
compliment A compliment is a nice thing that someone says about someone or something. Compliment can also be used as a verb: *They paid him a lot of compliments.* *She complimented me on my roses.*	***complement*** If people or things complement each other, they have different qualities that go well together: *The dry wine complements this rich dish perfectly.*
counsellor A counsellor gives people advice, often on personal matters, as a job: *They went to see a marriage counsellor.*	***councillor*** A councillor is an official in a local council: *She was elected as a councillor last year.*
dependent Dependent is an *adjective*. If you are dependent on someone or something, you rely on them: *Their economy is very dependent on oil.*	***dependant*** Dependant is a *noun*. Your dependants are the people you are financially responsible for: *He has a large income and no dependants.*
discreet If you are discreet, you are careful to avoid attracting attention or revealing private information: *I made a few discreet inquiries about her.*	***discrete*** If things are discrete, they are not joined or connected in any way: *I met him on three discrete occasions.*

draft A draft of a piece of writing is a first, rough version of it: *He showed me the first draft of his story.*	***draught*** A draught is a current of air: *There's a draught coming in through that window.* Note that in American English, this is spelled 'draft'.
draw Draw is a *verb* meaning to make a picture with a pencil: *Shall we draw a picture?*	***drawer*** A drawer is part of a desk, cupboard, etc.: *I put the papers away in a drawer.*
everyone Everyone is a pronoun and always refers to people: *Everyone enjoyed the show.*	***every one*** In the phrase 'every one', 'one' is a pronoun or a determiner that can refer to a person or a thing, depending on the context: *They have talked to every one of my classmates.* *We have eaten every one of the biscuits.*
hoard If you hoard things such as food or money, you save or store them for yourself: *She hoarded jars of fruit in the cellar.* Hoard can also be a *noun*: *We found a hoard of guns under the floorboards.*	***horde*** A horde is a large crowd of people: *Hordes of shoppers crowded outside the store.*
hole A hole is an opening or a hollow space in something: *There's a hole in my shoe.*	***whole*** Whole is a quantifier meaning 'all of something': *He ate the whole loaf.*

its Its means 'belonging to it': *The dog wagged its tail.*	***it's*** it's means 'it is' *It's going to be difficult to fit in all this work.*
led Led is the past participle of the verb 'lead': *He led me into a small room.*	***lead*** Lead is a *noun*, meaning 'a soft, grey metal': *The roof is covered with lead.* Lead is also a *verb*, but it has a different pronunciation.
licence Licence is a *noun*: *I showed him my driving licence.*	***license*** License is a *verb*: *We are not licensed to serve alcohol.* Note that in American English, *licence* is used for the verb and the noun.
pedal Pedal is a *noun* meaning the part of a bike you press with your foot, or a *verb* meaning to press that part: *Put your foot on the pedal.* *You'll have to pedal harder.*	***peddle*** If you peddle something, you sell it: *He was caught peddling drugs.*
practice Practice is a *noun*: *I did my piano practice.*	***practise*** Practise is a verb: *I practised the piano.* Note that in American English, *practice* is used for the verb and the noun.

principle Principle is a *noun* meaning 'a belief about what is right or wrong' or 'a basic rule': *Eating meat is against my principles.* *We learned the basic principles of yoga.*	***principal*** Principal is an *adjective* meaning 'most important': *Bad weather was the principal reason for the failure of the expedition.* Principal can also be a noun meaning 'the person in charge of a school or college': *She was sent to the principal's office.*
site A site is an area that is used for a particular purpose or where something happens: *He works on a building site.* *This is the site of the explosion.*	***sight*** Sight is the ability to see, and a sight is something you can see: *She lost her sight in an accident.* *I faint at the sight of blood.*
stationery Stationery is a *noun* meaning 'paper, envelopes and writing equipment': *Envelopes are kept in the stationery cupboard.*	***stationary*** Stationary is an *adjective* meaning 'not moving': *I drove into a stationary vehicle.*
story A story is something you read in a book: *I bought a book of fairy stories.*	***storey*** A storey is a level of a building: *My office is in a six storey building.*
whether Whether is a *conjunction* used to talk about a choice or doubt between two or more alternative: *I can't decide whether to have soup or salad.*	***weather*** Weather is a *noun* we use to talk about rain, snow, sun, etc.: *The weather was great in Portugal.*

whose Whose is a *pronoun* and a *determiner* used to ask questions about who something belongs to, or to talk about things connected to a particular person: *Whose shoes are these?* *He helped a woman whose face was covered with blood.*	***who's*** Who's means 'who is': *Who's going to do the washing up?*
witch Witch is a *noun*, meaning an evil magic woman: *We painted a witch on a broomstick.*	***which*** Which is a *pronoun* and a *determiner* used to ask questions when there are two or more possible alternatives, or to talk about things connected to a particular person: *Which is your cabin?* *I took the coat which looked warmest.*
your Your is a *pronoun* showing that something belongs to you or relates to you: *Where is your car?*	***you're*** You're means 'you are': *You're late again.*

Other words that are often confused

These words do not sound the same, but they are spelled in quite a similar way, and often cause confusion:

accept Accept is a *verb* and means 'agree to have': *I cannot accept money from you.*	***except*** Except is a *preposition* and a *conjunction* meaning 'not including': *Everyone was invited except Flora.*
adverse Adverse is a formal *adjective* meaning 'bad' or 'negative': *Do not attempt the climb in adverse weather conditions.*	***averse*** If you are averse to something, you do not like it: *I'm not averse to a sing-song now and then.*
advice Advice is a *noun*: *Can you give me some advice about growing roses?*	***advise*** Advise is a *verb*: *I advised him to wait a bit longer.*
beside Beside means 'next to': *Put the chair beside the window.*	***besides*** Besides means 'as well' or 'in addition to': *I don't need any help. Besides, I've nearly finished.* *He designed houses, office blocks, and much else besides.*
censure Censure is a formal verb, meaning 'to criticize strongly'. It is also a noun meaning the criticism: *They were censured for their failure to implement safety measures.* *The company received censure for its poor safety record.*	***censor*** Censor is a verb meaning 'to cut out parts of speech or writing'. It is also a noun meaning the person who does this: *His letters home from the war were heavily censored.* *Government censors cut out much of what he wrote.*

continual Continual is used to mean that something happens without interruption, and also that something happens repeatedly: *I'm fed up with this continual noise.* *There have been continual demands for action.*	***continuous*** Continuous is only used for things that happen without interruption and do not stop at all: *He has a continuous buzzing sound in his ear.*
definite If something is definite, it is firm and clear and not likely to be changed: *Do we have a definite date for the meeting?*	***definitive*** Something that is definitive provides a firm, unquestionable conclusion: *No one has come up with a definitive answer.*
dessert A dessert is the sweet dish you eat at the end of a meal: *Shall we have a dessert?*	***desert*** A desert is a large, dry sandy area: *We travelled through the Sahara Desert.*
elder Elder is used when you are saying which of two people was born first. It is not used with *than*: *I live with my elder sister.* *He is the elder of the two.*	***older*** Older simply means 'more old', and can be used of people or things, and can be followed by *than*: *My car is older than yours.*
flout If you flout a law or a rule, you do not obey it: *He accused the president of flouting international law.*	***flaunt*** If you flaunt something, you show it off in an obvious way: *I saw her at the party, flaunting her jewellery.*

infer If you infer something, you draw a conclusion from what you have seen, heard or read: *From his resignation letter, I inferred that he had been forced to leave.*	***imply*** If you imply something, you say it in an indirect way: *She implied that he owed her money.*
lay Lay is a *transitive* verb meaning 'to put something somewhere carefully', and must have an object: *Mothers often lay babies on their backs to sleep.* It is not correct to say 'I'm going to lay down' – you should use *lie* for this. Lay is also the past tense of *lie*: *We lay on the floor.*	***lie*** Lie is an *intransitive* verb meaning 'to be in a horizontal position': *I want to lie down.*
loose Loose is an *adjective* meaning 'not firmly fixed': *The bolts had worked loose.*	***lose*** Lose is a *verb* meaning 'to not have something any more' or 'to be defeated': *I'm always losing my keys.* *I think we're going to lose the match.*
personal Personal is an *adjective* meaning 'private' or 'relating to a particular person': *He asked me some very personal questions.* *She has her own personal helicopter.*	***personnel*** Personnel is a *noun* meaning 'the people who work in an organization': *All military personnel must report to base.*

quite Quite is an *adverb* and used to mean 'very' in a less emphatic way: *It was quite expensive.*	***quiet*** Quiet is an *adjective* and describes things or people that do not make much noise: *She had a very quiet voice.*

These groups of three words are among the most commonly misused words in English. They are all extremely frequent, so it is important that you are confident about using them correctly.

they're	They're means 'they are': *They're going to come on the train, I'll be angry if they're late again.*
their	Their is the possessive pronoun from 'they': *They forgot to bring their coats.* *Their faces were white and tear-stained.*
there	There is a pronoun and adverb used to show position or direction, to show that something exists, and at the beginning of many sentences and phrases: *There's your jacket.* *Can you see the lion over there?* *The old buildings are still there today.* *There must be another way of doing this.* *There are three churches in our town.*
too	Too is used before adjectives to mean 'more than is good': *It's too hot in here.* It also means 'as well': *I want some too.*

to	To is a preposition that is used in many ways, but the main ones are showing direction, showing who receives something, and forming the infinitive: *We went to the zoo.* *I gave it to John.* *I need to buy a new coat.*
two	Two is the number 2: *I have two brothers.*
we're	We're means 'we are': *We're having a party.* *I'll phone you when we're there.*
were	Were is the past tense of *be* when the subject is plural: *We were very happy.* *They were going to tell you.*
where	Where is used to talk about the location of things or to ask questions about the location of things: *Where do you live?* *I left the keys where Kabelo would be sure to find them.*

Words that are often spelled wrongly

These are words which people often misspell. A few of them are difficult words, but most of them are quite common, and it is important to spell them correctly.

accidentally	Don't forget *-ally* at the end, not just -ly.
accommodation	Double *c* and double *m*. This is one of the most commonly misspelled words in English.
acquire	Don't forget the *c* before the *q*.
advertisement	Don't forget the *e* after the *s*.
apparent	Double *p* but only one *r*.
beautiful	Learn the group of vowels – *eau* – at the beginning.
because	Remember *au* after the *c*.
believe	Remember *ie*, not ei.
Britain	Don't forget the *i* in the second syllable.
Caribbean	Only one *r*, but double *b*.
catastrophe	Unusually for English, the final *e* is pronounced, but remember it is only one *e* – don't be tempted to write y or ee.
category	Remember it's *e* in the middle, not i or a.
definite/definitely	Remember that there are two *i*'s and no a's in this word.
different	Double *f* and don't forget the *e* after them.

discipline	Don't forget the *c* after the *s* or the *e* at the end.
embarrassing	Double *r* and double *s*.
encyclopaedia or ***encyclopedia***	Formerly, British English used the first of these spellings, but the second is now used commonly. American English uses *encyclopedia*.
environment	Don't forget the *n* in the middle of this word.
especially	Remember that this word starts with *e*.
existence	This word ends *-ence*, not *-ance*.
favourite	Don't forget the *u* in the middle of this word. However, in American English, this word is spelled *favorite*.
foreign	Remember *ei* in the second syllable, and don't forget the *g*.
forty	Unlike *four*, there is no *u* in this word.
gauge	Remember the vowel sound is *au*.
government	Don't forget the *n* in the middle of this word. Remember that it comes from the word 'govern'.
grammar	Remember that this word ends *-ar*, not -er.
guarantee	Remember the *u* in the first syllable of this word.
independent	Remember that this word ends *-ent*, not -ant.
island	Don't forget the *s*.

leisure	Remember that in this word, *e* comes before *i*, which is the other way round from the usual rule.
library	Don't forget the *r* after the *b*.
lightning	Do not be tempted to add an e after *light*.
manoeuvre	The British spelling of this word (both the noun and the verb) has the complicated set of vowels *oeu* in it. The American English spelling of this word is *maneuver*.
mediaeval or ***medieval***	Formerly, British English used the first of these spellings, but the second is now used commonly. American English uses *medieval*.
millennium	Double *l* and double *n*.
miniature	Don't forget the second *i*.
minuscule	Note that the second vowel is *u*, not i. Try to think of it as beginning with *minus-*, not mini-
occurrence	Double *c* and double *r*.
opportunity	Double *p* and don't forget the *r* before the *t*.
possess/possession	Two lots of double *s*.
privilege	Remember that the middle vowel is *i*, and the last vowel is *e*. There are no a's in this word.
profession/professional/ professor	Remember there is only one *f* in these words.

pronunciation	Do not be tempted to add an *o* in the second syllable.
questionnaire	Remember to write double *n* in the middle.
receipt	Remember *ei* in the second syllable, and don't forget the silent *p*.
receive	Remember *ei* in the second syllable.
recommend	Only one *c* but double *m*.
relevant	Remember that the second vowel is *e*, not a.
restaurant	Remember to write *au* after the first *t*.
seize	Remember *ei*, here not ie.
separate	Remember that the second vowel is *a*, not e.
truly	Do not be tempted to add an e after *tru*.
weird	Remember *ei*, not ie.

Common mistakes and controversial issues

The English language arouses strong emotions. Many people have very fixed ideas about what is 'wrong' and what is 'right'. It is important when you write – apart from in very informal texts, emails, etc. – that you use a correct, standard form of English.

If you make mistakes such as putting apostrophes in the wrong place, or using the wrong form of a verb, your readers might be distracted from your message, and even take it less seriously.

It is important to remember that there are different customs for written and spoken English. While it might be acceptable in some situations to say something like, '*Jane and me are going to the shops*', non-standard uses should be avoided in writing.

Several customs of English grammar have come about as a result of people applying the grammar of Latin to English. However, many people are inconsistent about this. For instance, someone who objects to the use of the word *data* as a singular noun (because it is plural in Latin), may be quite happy to use the words *agenda* and *stamina* as singular nouns, even though they are Latin plurals too.

Another important thing to bear in mind is that language changes. The language used by EM Forster writing in the 20th century is very different from that of Shakespeare writing in the 16th century, but nobody would say that Forster's English was incorrect.

New words and phrases come into the language all the time, and even the grammar and structure of our sentences changes. Of course, British English is influenced by American English, and although some people dislike this, others pick up new usages with enthusiasm. For instance when asked '*How are you?*', many British people would now say '*Good, thanks*', or even '*I'm good*', which would not have been heard before the beginning of this century.

In the notes that follow, you will find guidance on what is acceptable and what is not acceptable in current British English. However, there are many issues where people disagree, and as always, it is important to think of your audience. For instance, many people do not care about split infinitives – in fact most people do not know what a split infinitive is! Nevertheless, if your writing is very formal, very important, or will be read by someone you know has very strict views on grammar, it may be best to avoid them.

All right or alright?

Some people consider that *alright* is not a 'real' word, and that *all right* should always be used. However, *alright* is very commonly used, particularly when representing speech. It may be best to avoid it in very formal writing.

Among or amongst?

Some people make the distinction that *among* is used when there is no movement and *amongst* when there is movement:

> *I stood among the crowd.*
> *We walked amongst the sand dunes.*

However, in modern English, is it not usual to make this distinction.

Among or between?

If we are talking, for example, of dividing or sharing things, *between* is usually used when there are only two people or things, and *among* when there are more than two:

Noma and Doyin shared the bread between them.
We distributed leaflets among the crowd.

Between is used after the verb *choose* no matter how many things there are:

It is difficult to choose between all the different styles.

Amount and quantity

In formal writing, it is best to use these nouns only with uncountable or mass nouns:

There was a large amount of mud on the carpet.
We bought a small quantity of gold.

It is not good style in formal writing to say things like: *I've got a huge amount of apples*. For countable nouns, it is best to use *number*, or to re-phrase the sentence, for example: *I've got a lot of apples*.

Comprise

Comprise is a rather formal word, and should not be used with the preposition *of*, even though the similar words *consist* or *be composed* are followed by *of*:

The grounds comprise a large lawn and 20 acres of woodland.
My cold remedy consists of lemon, honey and garlic.
The committee is composed of members of the legal profession.

Concerning

It is common to see concerning used as an adjective meaning 'worrying'. However, this use of concerning is not shown in most dictionaries, and must be considered non-standard. Concerning should be used only as a preposition:

She wrote to me concerning the new building work.

Could of/should of, etc.

It is a very common error to use *of* after modal verbs such as could, might, should or would. This is because in speech, it sounds as if that is what we are saying. However, the sound is really a weak form of the verb *have*, and this should always be used in writing:

We could have helped you if you had asked.
You should have called for a taxi.

Dangling participles

Dangling participles occur when the subject of the main clause is not the subject of the modifying clause that contains a participle (usually a word ending in *-ing* or *-ed*).

Look at the following sentence:

Coming home from work, my hat blew off.

Coming is a dangling participle here because its subject is not *my hat*. In formal writing, it would be better to say something like:

As I was coming home from work, my hat blew off.

Here is an example of a dangling past participle:

Loathed by his colleagues, we understood why he had been sacked.

This is incorrect in formal writing, because the subject of the main clause is 'we', but the subject of the participle is 'he'. It would be better to write something like:

He was loathed by his colleagues, so we understood why he had been sacked.

It is fine to use clauses with participles as long as the subject of the main clause matches:

Having seen the play before, I was keen to go again.

Data

Strictly speaking, data is the plural form of the Latin *datum*. Some people insist that it should be used with a plural verb:

The data were collected over several years.

However, data is increasingly being used as a singular noun, and most people would accept that as a valid modern use. There is some logic to this too, since data is often used as a synonym for *information* or *evidence*, which would take singular verbs:

All the data was uploaded to the new server.

Data tends to be used as a plural more commonly in scientific or academic writing. Whether you decide to use a singular or a plural verb with data, make sure that you are consistent throughout your document.

Decimate

This word originated from the Roman custom of killing one in ten of a group of soldiers guilty of crimes such as mutiny. A few people, therefore, prefer to use decimate very specifically to mean 'to reduce by one tenth'.

However, in modern English, decimate is used to mean 'to destroy a large amount or number of something', and this is widely acceptable:

Troops were decimated by illness.

Note that it is best not to use decimate – as many people do – to mean 'to destroy completely'. It is better to use a word like *destroy* or *annihilate* for this.

Different

The safest preposition to use with different is *from*, which is the same use as the related verb *differ from*:

These biscuits taste different from the other ones.

It is also considered acceptable in British, but not American English to use *to*:

Your circumstances are different to mine.

In American English, but not British English, *than* can be used:

He has a different job than me.

Dilemma

The word dilemma comes from the Greek prefix *di-* meaning 'two'. Therefore, purists argue that it should only be used to describe a situation where there are two alternatives, and not where there are a wider range of alternatives:

> *To support my husband or my son: that was my dilemma.*

In formal writing, dilemma should not be used simply as a synonym of 'problem', but only for situations where some sort of choice or decision is to be made.

Because the original Greek word referred to two unpleasant alternatives, some people also believe that it should still only be used in this way, and not for a choice between two pleasant things.

Disinterested or uninterested?

In formal, modern English, uninterested is used to mean 'not interested' and disinterested to mean 'unbiased' or 'impartial':

> *The audience seemed completely uninterested in what she had to say.*
> *We need a disinterested person to make a decision for us.*

However, in reality, the two words are used so interchangeably that even if you try to make the distinction, it is probably best to avoid 'disinterested' altogether to avoid ambiguity, and use *unbiased* or *impartial* instead.

Double negatives

A double negative is the use of two negative words in the same sentence. These are common in some dialects of spoken English, but should never be used in writing.

> *I haven't got no money.* (double negative)
> *I haven't got any money.* (standard English)
> *She didn't tell me nothing.* (double negative)
> *She didn't tell me anything.* (standard English)

Due to or owing to

Some people make a distinction between these two because *due* is an adjective and should therefore be used with a noun, and not a verb or a clause, where it is better to use *owing to*. A simple way to remember the difference is that *due to* can be replaced by *caused by* and *owing to* can be replaced by *because of*:

> *His illness was due to stress at work.*
> *Owing to the weather, the plane could not take off.*

Equally

It is common to see sentences such as the following:

> *Their work was equally as good.*
> *His house is equally as large as Ava's.*

However, in formal English, you should not use the word *as* with equally. Equally should come directly before the adjective:

> *Their work was equally good.*
> *His house and Ava's house are equally large.*

Farther/farthest or further/furthest?

The simplest rule is to use further/furthest all the time. A few people prefer to use farther when they are talking about literal distances:

We travelled farther into the mountains.

However, very few people make that distinction nowadays, and further is almost always used in more figurative senses:

We agreed to race to the furthest tree.
Let's pause to reflect before going any further with our discussion.

Fewer or less?

For people who are strict about grammar, fewer should be used before plural nouns and less before uncountable nouns:

There are fewer pupils in her class than last year.
I hope you'll have fewer problems this time.
I'm trying to use less butter in my cooking.
I had even less information about it than you.

In formal writing, it is best to stick to this rule, but in more informal contexts it is common to see less used before plural nouns:

There were less people there than I expected.
This checkout is for people with 10 items or less.

It is acceptable even in formal English to use less before numbers:

I had seen him less than five times in my life.

Hopefully

In current English it is extremely common to see the word hopefully used to mean 'it is hoped', usually at the beginning of a sentence:

> *Hopefully we won't have to wait long.*
> *Hopefully they'll pay us for the time we spent.*

However, some people object to this, saying that hopefully should only be used to mean 'in a hopeful way':

> *He looked at her hopefully.*
> *We waited hopefully to see if she would appear.*

It is best to stick to this second use in very formal writing.

I or me?

You should avoid writing sentences such as *Tim and me cooked a meal*.

When you use two pronouns or a personal name and a pronoun together, think about whether they are the subject or the object of the sentence:

> *Tom and I went to the football match.* (subject)
> *He asked Jo and me to sweep all the floors.* (object)

If you are not sure whether to use I or me, imagine you were only writing about yourself and not the other person. For instance, you would say *I went to the football match*, so that is the form to use when you add the other person too.

Irregardless

This is not a word in standard English, so do not use it in your writing. The word you need is *regardless*.

Lend or borrow

If you lend someone something, you let them use it for a while. If you borrow something, you take it from someone else to use for a while:

> *Can you lend me a pen?*
> *Can I borrow your pen?*

Literally

This word should be used only to emphasize that what follows is exact fact, and is not being said in an exaggerated or figurative way:

> *The waves were literally as high as a house.*
> *She was literally penniless.*

It is common for literally to be used simply to emphasize what follows, but examples like this should be avoided in formal writing:

> *I literally jumped out of my skin.*
> *Their eyes were literally out on stalks.*

Media

Strictly speaking, media is the plural form of the Latin *medium*. Some people insist that it should be used with a plural verb:

> *The media were guilty of invading her privacy.*

However, media is often used as a singular noun in current English:

The media is making the most of this scandal.

However, if you want to talk about one particular form of communication, you should use the singular *medium*:

She is of the view that television is a dangerous medium.

Off

The preposition off should not be followed by of:

It fell off of the table. (incorrect)
It fell off the table. (correct)

In other cases where 'off of' is used in spoken or non-standard English, the preposition *from* should be used:

I got it off of a friend of mine.
I got it from a friend.

Ought

Unlike with the other modal verbs (can, might, must, etc.), when you make questions and negatives with ought, it is necessary to add *to*. The use of ought in questions and negatives sounds quite formal:

Ought he to have gone?
Oughtn't we to see if he's all right?
You ought not to leave your keys in the door.

Out

The word out is an adverb:

I dropped my bag and all my money fell out.
I'm not going to go out today.

In standard, written English, if you want to use it as a preposition, you have to add *of*:

She threw the bag out of the window.
I walked out of the room.

Phenomena

Remember that phenomena is the plural of phenomenon. Do not use phenomena as a singular:

Lightning is a natural phenomena. (incorrect)
Lightning is a natural phenomenon. (correct)

The reason being

Do not use the verb 'is' after this phrase, because it does not relate grammatically. You should use **that**:

We had to sell the business, the reason being that my husband was ill.

Refute

This word is often used simply to mean 'deny', but this is not correct, standard use. Refute means to prove something wrong with evidence.

With these documents, he was able to refute the allegations.

Sat

Avoid sentences such as *I was sat on the floor*. This is not a grammatically correct tense because we do not use a past participle after *was* or *were*. Instead, you should write:

I was sitting on the floor.

Split infinitives

A split infinitive is where you write an adverb between *to* and a verb, e.g. *to finally agree*.

A lot of people do not like this, although plenty of great writers such as Donne, Eliot and Browning have used it. In very formal writing, it is best to re-order your words:

We were asked to carefully look inside the box. (split infinitive)
We were asked to look carefully inside the box.

In a few cases, a split infinitive is necessary to avoid a change in meaning:

He failed to completely understand my point.
(split infinitive, but means that he did not understand everything about the point)

He completely failed to understand my point.
(this has a different meaning – that he was unable to understand the point at all)

He failed to understand my point completely.
(this could have either meaning, and is therefore ambiguous)

Try

In British English, it is acceptable to use *and* or *to* after try, though *and* is slightly less formal:

Try and find the coin.
We will try to help you.

In American English, *try and* is not considered correct.

Used to

Note that when using the negative and question forms with used to, you need to drop the *d* from *used*:

Years ago, children used to be more polite.
I used to hate broccoli, but now I like it.
Children didn't use to have TVs in their bedrooms.
Did you use to play football when you were a child?

In a very formal style, we could write:

I used not to have a car.
I usedn't to need glasses.

While or whilst?

These two words are used in the same way in British English.

I read a book while I was waiting.
Whilst she slept, I cooked a meal.

In American English, while is used.

Who or whom?

Who is now commonly used as the object where in the past it was only considered correct to use whom:

Who do you work for?

If you use whom in sentences like this, your writing will sound extremely formal:

For whom do you work?

However, you must use whom directly after a preposition:

The woman to whom I spoke was a local nurse.
There were twenty masked prisoners, many of whom were armed.

Index